Syria

SUNY Series in Middle Eastern Studies

Shahrough Akhavi, Editor

Syria

Society, Culture, and Polity

Edited by
Richard T. Antoun and Donald Quataert

STATE UNIVERSITY OF NEW YORK PRESS

Published by
State University of New York Press, Albany

© 1991 State University of New York

For information, address State University of New York
Press, State University Plaza, Albany, N.Y. 12246

Production by Dana Foote
Marketing by Fran Keneston

Library of Congress Cataloging in Publication Data

Syria : Society, Culture, and Polity / edited by Richard T. Antoun and
   Donald Quataert.
      p. cm. — (SUNY Series in Middle Eastern Studies)
   The product of a conference held in 1987 at the State University
of New York—Binghamton, sponsored by the Southwest Asian and North
African Studies Program.
   Includes bibliographical references (p.) and index.
   ISBN 0-7914-0713-6 (cloth : alk. paper). — ISBN 0-7914-0714-4
(paper : alk. paper)
   1. Syria—Congresses. I. Antoun, Richard T. II. Quataert,
Donald, 1941–   . III. State University of New York at Binghamton.
Program in Southwest Asian and North African Studies. IV. Series.
DS92.3.S97   1991
956.91—dc20   90-10251
                                              CIP

10 9 8 7 6 5 4 3 2 1

CONTENTS

PREFACE

Donald Quataert

In April 1987 the Southwest Asian and North African Studies Program (SWANA) sponsored a conference, "Syria: The Society, Culture, and Polity of a Complex Middle Eastern Nation," held on the campus of the State University of New York at Binghamton. The present book is a product of that effort, assembled by two editors. The first is a social anthropologist, Richard Antoun; the second, Donald Quataert, is a historian of the Ottoman Empire. As we all know, social anthropologists study present behavior and historians examine the past. But this book inverts the natural order; it permits the historian the first word on past events, then the anthropologist's insights through contemporary field research.

Syria clearly is a significant country. It is both a region of major historical consequence and a modern state, playing a vital role in regional and global politics. The area occupied by the modern Syrian state long has been an experimental laboratory in areas of life as diverse as religion and politics. After all, Saul/Paul had his religious crisis on the road to Damascus. It is a less well-known fact that, approximately a thousand years later, the region nurtured the rise of the Druze faith. In the twentieth century, its environment promoted the emergence of Arab nationalism, and later the Ba'th Party, an Arab–Middle Eastern variant on socialism. The ecology of its mountains still shelters a few speakers of millennia-old languages otherwise vanished, while the economy of its plains are now transforming honored tribal patterns of existence. Few would argue against the contemporary importance of Syria. It stands in the center of Arab politics and for years was the coveted prize of Pan-Arab unification schemes. The Ba'th Party born on its soil continues to be important in the political life of the wider Arab world. Syria plays a key role in the major international problems of the area, variously promoting or impeding resolution of the Arab-Israeli and Lebanese crises.

For all its rich diversity and importance, however, the country has been the focus of remarkably little attention by scholars. As any survey of the bibliographic literature will demonstrate, there are comparatively very few articles and books on modern-day Syria. It was this sharp contrast between Syrian significance and the scarcity of relevant literature that initially attracted the attention of the editors, prompting the conference and now this volume.

Individuals and nations alike are shaped by their past, and modern-day Syria is no exception. In the post-Ottoman, post-French twentieth century, Syrians have embarked on a new course of identity formation and political organization. But in important ways, the Syrian past constrains, restricts, shapes, and traps. Its historic economy profoundly was affected by the post-World War I boundaries agreed upon by France and Britain. One stroke of a pen on the map severed the great manufacturing center of Aleppo from both its suppliers and its customers to the north, in the region that became the republic of Turkey. Another line created the Mandate and later the state of Lebanon, formalizing a barrier between the Mediterranean Sea and the Syrian caravan cities of Aleppo, Homs, Hama, and Damascus. The Syrian economy has since wrestled with these demarcations. Syrian policymakers, for their part, remain drawn to Lebanon. The pull of the past, however, is not irresistible and should not be overstated. If Lebanon seems alluring to Syrian leaders, other historically Syrian regions lost to the modern state at the hands of foreign mapmakers do not. In 1938, France gave the Syrian district of Alexandretta to the Turkish republic in a ploy to win support in the imminent World War II. Despite this, there are few efforts to regain the lost district. Lebanese weakness and Turkish strength and not simply Syrian history seem relevant in understanding Syrian irredentism (or its absence).

The contribution by Philip S. Khoury (and his 1987 book on Syria and the French Mandate) exemplifies a major, new, and healthy development in Middle East studies: an acknowledgment of the Ottoman past as important to the contemporary Middle East. This is a radical shift, although Albert Hourani pointed the way many years ago in his 1969 pamphlet, "The Ottoman Background to the Modern Middle East." With this exception, scholars, journalists, and diplomats wrote of the twentieth-century Arab Middle East as if it were a tabula rasa. For these new Arab states (as for Turkey), the immediate past—that is, the Ottoman experience—was irrelevant, except as an obstacle to be overcome, a dead hand. It was seen to have no significance or impact on modern Arab (or Turkish) life. Khoury's efforts are an important addition to a growing body of work that corrects this wrongheaded view and treats the Ottoman past for what it is, an integral part of modern Middle East life.

Other studies in this emerging pattern include Hanna Batatu's epochal work on Iraq and William Cleveland's fine books on Sati al-Husri and Shakib Arslan, as well as Haim Gerber's fascinating (if flawed) study of Middle East landholding patterns. Sulayman Khalaf's article in this volume, for its part, is intimately tied to Norman Lewis's book on nineteenth-century tribal sedentarization patterns in Syria. The two should be read together to see how intimately the Syrian past folds into the present. All these studies make clear the relevance of the Ottoman past for the modern Arab world.

In its parts, the present volume also offers studies of the state and its role in shaping society and of the Alawis, their beliefs and their political role. Other sections examine Asad and Syrian-Soviet relations. Between these covers are contributions from a variety of disciplines and backgrounds, including anthropology, political science, history, journalism, language, and literature. In its multidisciplinary richness, this is an unusual book. Further, it strikes a fine balance between synopsis and minute analysis. On the heights, there are the synoptical chapters of Philip Khoury, Hinnebusch, and Seale while closer to the ground are the microstudies of Khuri, Khalaf, Cobban, and Altoma. All together, the book offers a richly textured entree to a fascinating subject.

NOTE ON TRANSLITERATION

Since this book is aimed at the general, informed reading public as well as at academics and area specialists, the editors have chosen to simplify the orthography and transliteration of Arabic words and phrases. Long marks over Arabic vowels have been omitted and an apostrophe has been used to designate the 'ayn as well as the hamzah. Arabic words in common usage have not been italicized. Arabic words are italicized only where they refer to key concepts pertaining to religious ideology.

Brief Chronology of Syrian History

1516	Ottoman conquest of Syria
1799	Unsuccessful invasion of Syria by Napoleon Bonaparte
1833	Muhammad Ali Pasha of Egypt occupies Syria
1839	Ottomans resume control
1839	Hatt-i Sherif of Gulhane reform decree
1856	Hatt-i Humayun reform decree
1908	Young Turk revolution and restoration of 1876 Ottoman Constitution
1914	Ottoman Empire declares war on Britain and France
1917	Collapse of Ottoman authority in Syria
1920	Independent Arab state of Syria declared but defeated by France and Britain
1922	Formal mandate for Syria (and Lebanon) held by France begins
1925	Insurrection of the Druze
1936	French-Syrian agreement to end Mandate in three years
1939	France enters World War II and delays end of Mandate
1941	Syria formally becomes an independent nation
1946	Syria actually becomes an independent nation with French withdrawal
1958–1961	Syria part of abortive United Arab Republic with Egypt
1970	Asad becomes president of Syria

GLOSSARY

Arabic Words and Specialized Terms

acculturation   the process of the borrowing of cultural traits without a change of identity of the borrowing group

Alawis   a religious sect with historical Muslim roots but distinctive theological beliefs, concentrated in the Latakia region of Syria

'asabiyya   the power of social solidarity; originally referring to the social solidarity and *esprit de corps* of tribal groups in the Middle East; now extended to the solidarity of groups generally

ashraf   families claiming descent from the prophet, Muhammad

assimilation   the process of absorption of cultural traits along with their underlying values, therefore entailing change of identity

Ba'th (Party)   the ruling party of Syria since 1963 whose ideology combines Arab nationalism, Arab unity, and socialism

bab   "gate"; among the Alawis a religious leader possessed of esoteric, sacramental knowledge who is sometimes a public figure and sometimes hidden

comprador (bourgeois)   elements of the indigenous population, usually minorities, associated closely with foreign capital

confessionalism   referring to an ideology and society in which religious ties are invoked to advance personal or political ambitions

demarche   maneuver, diplomatic move

dhimmi(s)	the non-Muslim minorities within the monotheistic tradition (Christians, Jews, and Zoroastrians) granted religious tolerance by the Muslim state in return for political subordination
dyadic	relating to face-to-face, two-person relationships
fellah/fellahin	Arab peasant(s)
hadith	written tradition of the prophet
hectare	a measure of land composing approximately 2.5 acres in twentieth-century Syria
Ikhwan	"brothers"; in Syria and other Arab countries designating the Muslim Brotherhood, a religious movement and association that became increasingly hostile to the rule of Asad in the 1970s and 1980s
imam	prayer leader; Muslim religious leader; for the Alawis a divine, infallible source of will
Ismailis	distinctive Shi'a Muslim sect found in Pakistan, India, East Africa, and Syria, headed by the Agha Khan
Ithna 'Ashariyya	refers to the "twelver" school of Islamic law and, more generally, to the Shi'a Muslims of Iran, Iraq, and Lebanon
kilo	a unit of weight, approximately 2.2 pounds
khanji	Syrian broker, merchant, moneylender, caravansaray owner
kulakization	process of conversion of collective land and water resources to private ownership and control
lineage	a corporate kinship group that traces descent through a single line, in Syria through the father's line
Maronite	an individual from the dominant Christian sect in Lebanon
multiplex	cutting across many interests, referring to roles and relationships—for example, the father of the family may also be a mediator, a prayer leader, and a cultivator
muzari'	landowner, cultivator

neo-Ba'th	bureaucratically oriented government party associated with Asad's rise to power, particularly after his becoming president in 1970
patrimonial	a society in which the most prominent ties are personalistic, those between patrons and clients (rather than between classes or ethnic groups) who informally contract ties to receive rewards
sect	distinctive religious group with its own homeland and exclusive worldview (in the Middle East)
sectarianism	referring to an ideology and society in which religious ties define the leading social groups
sheikh/shaykh	elder; tribal leader (as in rural Syria); also religious leader; among Alawis the religious knowledge of the *shaykh* is esoteric and the position is usually hereditary
Shi'a	the largest sect in Islam, differing somewhat from the Sunni branch in law, theology, popular religious observance, and principles of political succession; the Shi'a are themselves divided into the *ithna 'ashariyya,* who live mainly in Iran, Iraq, and Lebanon, the Ismailis, who live in India, Pakistan, and East Africa, and the Zaydis, who live in Yemen
Sunni/s	referring to members of the largest and (in most countries) dominant Muslim religious community, differing in law, theology, popular religious observance, and principles of political succession from Shi'a Muslims; all Muslims, both Sunni and Shi'a, however, unite in their fundamental belief in the five pillars of Islam: profession of faith ("there is no god but God and Muhammad is the Messenger of God") prayer, fasting (the month of Ramadan), pilgrimage (to Mecca), and the giving of alms (*zakat*) to the needy
suq	market; bazaar; more broadly the merchant sector of the Syrian economy and polity
taqiyya	dissimulation; a tendency of certain ethnic and religious minorities to conceal their identity and acculturate publicly to the dominant culture

'ulema   the religious scholars of Islam, often composing an important part of local urban elites in the nineteenth century

umma   the Muslim community in a comprehensive social sense as distinguished from particular Muslim states

wasata   designates both the informal process of intermediation to secure a favor as well as the intermediary himself

za'im   leader; more specifically, a local or regional political boss who may or may not hold political office

Syria: Area and Population

AREA, POPULATION AND DENSITY

Area (sq km)	
Land	184,050
Inland Water	1,130
Total	185,180*
Population (census results)#	
23 September 1970	6,304,685
8 September 1981	
Males	4,624,761
Females	4,427,867
Total	9,052,628
Population (official estimates at mid-year)#	
1984	9,934,000
1985	10,268,000
1986	10,612,000
Density (per sq km) at mid-1986	57.3

* 71,498 sq miles

#Including Palesinian refugees, numbering 193,000 at mid-1977

PRINCIPAL TOWNS (population at 1981 census)

Damascus	1,112,214	Rakka	87,138
Aleppo	985,413	Hasakeh	73,426
Homs	346,871	Tartous	52,589
Latakia	196,791	Edleb	51,682
Hama	177,208	Dera'a	49,534
Deir ez-Zor	92,091	Suweidiya	43,414

ECONOMICALLY ACTIVE POPULATION* (sample survey, '000 persons aged 10 years and over, April 1984)

	Males	Females	Total
Agriculture, hunting, forestry and fishing	429.3	142.5	571.7
Mining and quarrying	17.4	0.3	17.7
Manufacturing	301.7	34.9	336.7
Electricity, gas and water	18.2	1.1	19.3
Construction	361.8	4.8	366.6
Trade, restaurants and hotels	243.4	9.4	252.9
Transport, storage and communications	122.6	5.1	127.7
Financing, insurance, real estate and business services	13.0	4.2	17.3
Community, social and personal services	438.5	98.0	536.5
Total Employed	1,945.9	300.4	2,246.3
Unemployed	82.8	26.8	109.6
Total labour force	2,028.8	327.2	2,356.0

*Figures refer to Syrian Arabs only, excluding armed forces.

SOURCE: The Annual Survey, The Middle East and North Africa 1989
Europa Publications, London, 1988

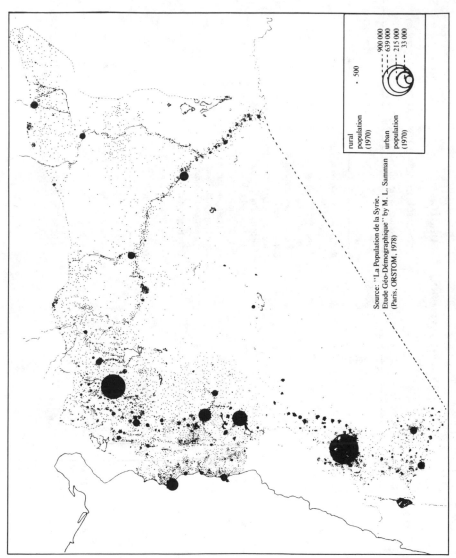

Source: "La Population de la Syrie.
Etude Géo-Démographique" by M. L. Samman
(Paris, ORSTOM, 1978)

rural population (1970)	· 500
urban population (1970)	900 000 639 000 215 000 33 000

Distribution of Population in Syria, 1970

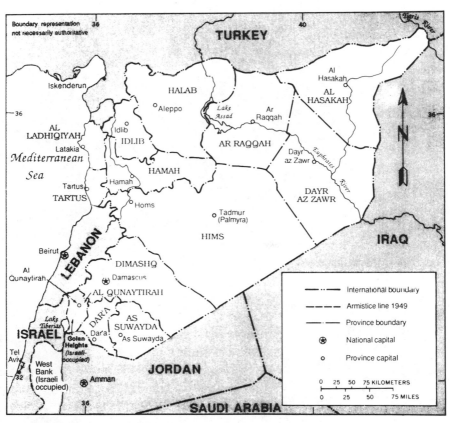

Modern Syria: Administrative Divisions

INTRODUCTION

Ethnicity, Clientship, and Class: Their Changing Meaning

Richard T. Antoun

Albert Hourani, a prominent historian of the modern Middle East has stated that "Even were there no Syrian people, a Syrian problem would still exist."[1] Syria's geographical and strategic position at the eastern end of the Mediterranean Sea and near the convergence of three continents established its political importance long ago. Hourani pointed out that, historically, Syria has served as a focus of political and economic movements, "at times as a starting-point, at others as a terminus or a bridge."[2] At a crossroads of world trade, it is not accidental that Syrian merchants, historically and today, play a prominent role in the economy and politics of the country. As a crossing ground for armies and caravans, at times a leading province in empires far larger than itself, it is remarkable that near the end of the twentieth century "the isolation of Syria" should appear so frequently as a theme in the writings of scholars and observers of the contemporary Syrian scene (see Cobban, this volume; and Sadowski 1987—n. 19).

The reaction of Syria's people to the contrasting cultural, demographic, economic, and political currents from across the Mediterranean and Europe on the one hand and across the desert and Arabia on the other, has been absorption and accommodation, and often at the same time tension and conflict. Accommodation has taken place at the sociocultural level in the development of a mosaic society well adapted to the geographical diversity of the country, in which a number of ethnic groups and sects (Sunni Muslims, Alawis, Druze, Greek Orthodox, Kurds, Circassians, Ismailis) find their niches in various regions of the country or in various ethnic divisions of labor in urban centers. Accommodation has taken place at the psychocultural level in "the art of rapid and superficial

1

assimilation and that of preserving, beneath new modes of behavior and in new forms, their old beliefs and ways of living.''[3] Flight to the peripheries, acculturation but not assimilation,[4] and dissimulation (*taqiyya*) have been alternative strategies pursued by Syrians for centuries.

The geographic diversity of Syria, and the existence of a sparse but ethnically diverse population divided by long distances and natural barriers (deserts and mountains), probably encouraged the development of specialization and trade (caravans) between separate centers. Coon sketched the lineaments of this mosaic model for the societies of the Middle East almost fifty years ago in his book *Caravan*.[5] For Coon, the pieces of the mosaic were ethnic groups, social types (e.g., villages, urban quarters, and nomad camps), communities specializing in regional products, and the "tame" (living in the plains under government control) and the "insolent" (tribesmen of the mountains and deserts). The basic units of the mosaic were large extended families and familylike groups (e.g., guilds and brotherhoods), which passed on scarce resources and rare skills endogamously within the ethnic group or social type. These skills were linked to a metal-age preindustrial level of hand-powered industry utilizing skilled hand-labor. The cement of the mosaic society was trade (and thus the high status of the merchant, bazaar, and caravan) integrating an ethnic division of labor, and Islam (prayer, fasting, pilgrimage, and Sufi orders) imposing a broad cultural-ritual uniformity on an otherwise diverse population characterized by differences in diet, dress, hairstyle, language, days of worship, and leisure activities.

In recent years infrastructural development, particularly in transportation, has linked all of Syria's major cities with one another and with its new, growing ports.[6] Such national economic integration is certainly in line with the policy of a regime guided by nationalist and socialist principles. But Syria's growing population (from 5.3 million in 1961 to 10.6 million in 1981) continues to reflect a pronounced and relatively stable regionalism: Damascus and Aleppo together comprised 42.9 percent of all Syrians in 1960 and 43.2 percent in 1981. Hama and Der'a, the provinces that grew the most in the interim, increased their share of the population by only one percent.[7] The seven largest cities in 1960 were still the seven largest in 1981. Moreover, Syria is not characterized by the typical Middle Eastern dominance of the single capital city (the primate pattern). Aleppo, though not as large as Damascus, is nearly as large, and Syria has several substantial medium-sized cities — Latakia, Homs, and Hama. Urbanization has proceeded apace in Syria as in the rest of the Middle East; Syrians living in cities increased from 37 percent in 1960 to 47 percent in 1981. However, the only provinces with an urban majority are Damascus, Aleppo, and Homs. The distribution of Syria's population, then, still indicates the relevance of the mosaic model for understanding Syrian society.

But there is another model,[8] quite different, that has been used to understand modern Syria: a medium-sized, neither rich nor poor, basically agricultural country subject to periodic drought. That model does not focus on geography, regionalism, ethnic diversity, or the enshrinement of such diversity in custom or ideology; rather, it focuses on class. This model assumes that modern Syrian society can be best understood by the assumption that deep-seated social dislocations have pitted one class against another: landlord vs. peasant, new, salaried middle class employed in army, bureaucracy, or schools vs. established urban merchants; and by the assumption that "capitalist" penetration erodes "clientelist" ties and sets off "proletarianization" of the peasantry. At a later stage the new elite becomes a shadowy state-formation and a spearhead of "embourgeoisement" (see Hinnebusch, this volume, for the argument). Political movements, then, rather than reflecting the ethnic and clientelist loyalties of a mosaic society, reflect the drive of an incipient elite (now a "class vanguard") propelled by a revolutionary doctrine to form a mass base, capture the state apparatus, and turn it to the ends of the dominant class (see Hinnebusch, this volume).

Is there any way of reconciling these models? Probably not, in their current formulations. But the refinement of either or both could lead to a better understanding of Syrian society. The remainder of this essay will explore some suggestions for refining competing frameworks. By exploring such frameworks it may be possible for scholars in the future to gain a better understanding of important institutions and processes of change in contemporary Syria: the changing Syrian family, political factionalism, the sedentarization of nomads, bureaucratic corruption, patron-client ties, the development/constriction of regionalism, the development of the Ba'th Party, rural-urban migration, religious resurgence, Syria's political isolation, and the continued importance of sects in contemporary Syrian life.

Before exploring the implications of such models for understanding Syria, I must sketch briefly a few of the significant stable contours of this society and recent changes in them. Syrian society since early Ottoman times has featured a military, land-holding elite that has managed affairs of state out of necessity by finding a partner in local urban notables, themselves composed of merchants on the one hand and religious (scholar) influentials on the other (see Khoury, this volume, for the argument). After the collapse of the Ottoman Empire at the end of World War I, this urban elite seized upon Arab nationalism as a means to solidify and legitimize power, and construct cross-regional, cross-class, and cross-ethnic alliances against French mandatory control. These elites, dominantly Sunni Muslim, developed considerable skills as mediators and interhierarchical leaders, articulating separate regional interests while maintaining their own dominance (see Khoury, this volume).

As a student of human geography, Weulersse has pointed out that this articulation was quite different than that which had prevailed in Western Europe in the preindustrial period. There were no old bourgeois families tracing their roots to the countryside, maintaining their ties with it, and often returning to it for economic and cultural sustenance. Rather, for much of Syrian history, cities were foreign bodies, indeed, often established by foreigners and in any case dominated by them: Seljuks, Mongols, Mamluks, Turks. The relationship between these cities and their rural hinterlands was basically exploitive, with the city/state taking much and returning little.[9]

On the other side, that of the Syrian peasantry living in diverse villages adapted to diverse microecological niches in varied environments, there was no love of the land, per se, as has been attributed to peasants in parts of the Nile Valley or to the peasants of France till modern times as, for instance, portrayed in the novels of Zola. Admittedly, here we are dealing with stereotypes of the peasantry constructed by historians, orientalists, social scientists, journalists and, not least, by the peasants themselves. Hence all statements about "peasant society and culture," particularly in the rapidly changing decades at the end of the twentieth century, are something less than half-truths. With this caveat in mind, we can still observe that in Syria the peasant often worked for absentee landlords or their agents for low rewards in an arid climate that was in any case uncertain, and produced modest to low crop yields. In these circumstances the peasant was often little enamored of rural life, and migration to towns or cities was seldom viewed as a tragedy. Should economic opportunity allow, he readily moved, and moves away from the countryside now, as the growing urbanization of Syria indicates.

If the stereotype of the sober, workmanlike peasant with "an intimate and reverent attitude toward the land" described by the anthropologist Redfield as the exemplar of the peasant ethos finds scant support in Syria, the fact remains that Syria has been and remains a fundamentally agricultural society.[10] As late as 1970 fifty percent of the Syrian labor force was employed in agriculture and seventy percent of all Syrian exports were agricultural products.[11] Although industry has grown substantially, most of it continues to be tied to agriculture; textiles and food processing. Farming of all kinds, including sheepraising, contributes a larger proportion of the GNP and supports more people than any other activity.[12] Of course, this agriculture has undergone substantial changes, chief among them the substantial control of much agricultural production by the state, determining what, when, with which credits, at what price, and in what markets crops could be produced and sold. The post-1961 land reforms left many wealthy landlords and tribal leaders relatively powerless, and gave other enterprising and peripheral groups an opportunity to gain a greater stake in both the land and the new revolutionary regime. Khalaf's essay (this volume) provides a good example of this process.

In addition, the state considerably widened the public sector in agriculture and undertook a number of development schemes closely supervised by the government, such as the Ghab irrigation project. The remarkable fact is that more than twenty-five years after a socialist regime has come to power in Syria, a regime that is theoretically in total control of the public sector, considerable private initiative is still allowed — in fact, 75 percent of the country's lands are in private hands — and within the state-controlled system of agriculture peasants mobilize successful efforts to gain access to an open-market economy. Metral has described in detail numerous peasant strategies within the government-run Ghab irrigation project to increase their access to the means of production in violation of formal development scheme rules: renting land illegally from neighbors to produce catch crops; hooking up siphons or pumps to canals to get extra water; securing protection for illegalities in the local scheme administration, the party, or the army; forming informal irrigation units to create large enough land units to contract with large machinery owners; and investing the profits of private agricultural enterprise into tractor, truck, and other petty enterprises. Moreover, these strategies reflect and accelerate certain pronounced tendencies in Syrian not-just-rural society: the regrouping of extended families and village (sect) mates in local areas; the diversification of income sources to crosscut agricultural, industrial, and service economies; and the extension of family networks to penetrate systems of state-run activities (ministries, Ba'th Party, army, schools).[13]

The Ghab irrigation project emphasizes the continuity of Syrian social processes and structures across time and through regimes of diverse ideological and class orientation — Ottoman, Mandate, nationalist, socialist: the importance of the extended family as a solidary unit bridging social categories (such as class, village/city, rulers/ruled); the continued importance of patron-client relations (now labeled *sharik* or "partner" relations in the Ghab area) in a nationalist-socialist state; and the persistence of "peasant" strategies of shrewdness, pragmatism, manipulation, and opportunism, not for the love of the land but rather to maximize economic opportunities.

Metral's analysis of the Ghab irrigation project points to the continuities of Syrian culture and social process, and the diversification of occupations in extended family units to gain access to a wider range of resources. Khalaf's essay (this volume), examining a quite different economic and social region of Syria, elaborates similar themes: the al-Meshrif family's diverse economic activities included sheep raising, dry cereal farming, rental of town property, and rental of land for cotton crops. Muhammad Meshrif himself became a *sharik* (here, moneylender) to the *fellahin* while at the same time gathering his own relatives to work the land. But Khalaf's analysis of land reform and class structure in the al-Raqqa region of northern Syria emphasizes other processes clearly related to the development of sharp social stratification, but not emphasized by Metral. The Meshrifs of al-Raqqa recruit other tribesmen (than their own) and nontribal *fellahin* as cultivators who begin to outnumber the kinsmen in their employ. A new rural elite, identified with city merchants and alienated from their own tribesmen, who come to be called "cotton sheikhs," emerge. These sheikhs cease to collect tribute from their tribal clients (gifts of lamb in the spring and grain at harvest). Afdala sheikhs drive Cadillacs and employ "slaves" as servants, build guest houses of cut stone with glass-paned windows. Stratification emerges between the *muzari'* (literally, "planter," but functionally, farmer-entrepreneur) and the peasants, and patron-client tribal ties lapse as the new rural bourgeois intensify marriage only among close kinsmen (and not distant) while buying more urban property and investing in the education of their children (see Khalaf, this volume). Lewis, a historian of modern Syria, has noted that client riverine tribes who take up irrigated agriculture along the Euphrates generally outstrip their patron Fid'an sheikhs in wealth, become politically active, and aspire to social equality.[14]

Khalaf's analysis raises the question posed above, about the refinement of class and mosaic models to better understand modern Syria. Longuenesse, in dealing with the Syrian working class today in a mainly industrial, urban context, Hinnebusch (this volume), in dealing with class in relation to the development of the Ba'thist state, and Lewis, in dealing with the settlement of the frontier in Greater Syria from 1800 to 1980, have stressed certain themes that make strict application of a class model problematic. Longuenesse, for instance, points to the frequency of "moonlighting" among industrial workers in Syria. Clearly related to low wages, moonlighting in both public and private sectors combines such diverse occupations as factory-worker, itinerant salesman, farmer, artisan, and transporter of goods in a Suzuki mini-van.[15] Lewis, describing the modernization of shepherding along the desert margin, has stressed the incongruous but flexible and complex adaptive practices that have become common. Some Syrian beduin herd sheep for most of the year but travel to Saudi Arabia to work in construction or the oil fields in the winter; their richer relatives become businessmen there. Flocks owned by urban capitalists are cared for by shepherd families relying on vehicles for water and other supplies. Tribes living in huge handsome tents, specializing in the raising, running, and marketing of sheep, drive their own trucks, join cooperatives, and have social dealings with merchants in Palmyra, Aleppo, and Homs. Alongside them, poor beduin with meager flocks living in ragged goat hair tents and dressed in jeans commute in buses in order to work in phosphate mines.[16]

Hinnebusch (this volume) has pointed out that in modern Syria families operate as solidary social units bridging social categories (including class). Furthermore, the large informal sector with one foot in commerce and the other in white-collar government offices straddles other social categories, such as village and state. To add to the complicated and highly flexible and mobile character of contemporary Syrian social structure, which fact makes application of the usual categories of class analysis difficult, are the other attributes of the Syrian working class reported by Longuenesse: the high rate of turnover in both public and private sectors, and the resort not to labor organization and strikes as a form of worker resistance but rather to flight, migration (to the Arab Gulf) and self-employment.[17]

Battatu, in a preliminary fashion, tried to deal with some of the complexities, flexibilities, and mobilities of modern Syrian life; first, by distinguishing more precisely between categories of social analysis — that is, distinguishing between "family," "tribe," and "sect" in analyzing the power base of Syria's ruling military group; and second, by merging categories — using the term "sect-class" to indicate the existence of groups with ethnic labels (e.g., "Alawis," or in Iraq, "Takritis") that follow basically class interests. He argues that the Alawis until the 1950s cultivated the soil for middle-class Christian and Sunni Muslim landlords (of Latakia) or large landlords (of Akkar or Hama) for one-quarter of the crop, and were subject to the treatment appropriate to their class—revilement and indenture.[18]

Sadowski has attempted to refine the sense in which Syria is at the same time a patrimonial (rather than a class) and a mosaic society, first, by pointing out that the Alawis were never highly unified, with three cults and four tribes, in addition to division between factions, and between young and old, and second, by distinguishing between "sectarianism," which is not characteristic of current Syrian society, and "confessionalism," which is. He argues that "Alawis," and by implication others with ethnic identities, invoke relations with other Alawis to advance personal and ideological ambitions rather than to promote the common interests of the sect, and that "fealty is a far more important criterion than religion for the distribution of power in Syria." President Asad's *jama'a* or "inner circle" is composed of a number of Sunnis (Khaddam and Tlas), not to get "Sunni" support but rather because they are loyalists and intimate friends. Moreover, he argues that Asad does not promote Alawis in general but rather Alawis of his own tribe or more specifically, his own native village as well as his own close relatives (brothers, cousins, in-laws). Generally speaking he argues that patronage is a more important factor than ethnicity in analyzing contemporary Syrian political life, at least at the leadership level.[19]

A geographer, Drysdale, on the other hand, in a little noted but valuable (1979) article, has described briefly several models for understanding ethnicity in the Syrian officer corps and proposed his own refinement. The two main competing models, according to Drysdale, are what one might term the "patrimonial" and the "modernizing." The first describes the army in terms of a praetorian guard — that is, the army is a client to the patron (historically the emperor, but here the president of the republic), giving him its absolute loyalty and receiving appropriate largesse in return. Notions of autonomy, corporate identity, and professionalism are clearly inapplicable here. The second model describes the army in terms of universalistic norms applied to an autonomous, hierarchical, disciplined, professional, corporate group devoted to efficiency and capable of innovation. A third model largely associated with the work of the anthropologist Geertz is mentioned by Drysdale, but dismissed.[20] I term this model the "primordial." Illustrating with a number of cases including Malaya, Lebanon, and Morocco, Geertz argues that in the post–World War II era the formation of new nations in Asia and Africa created new, wider, and richer arenas for the competition for scarce resources. Ethnic groups including sects, tribes, and minorities (and often at the beginning of the process they were more ethnic categories than sociological groups), mobilized themselves as never before to compete more effectively in the national arena for these new scarce resources: irrigation water, land, schools, roads, factories, sanitation facilities, college degrees. The proliferation of national states led to the mobilization of ethnicity.[21]

Drysdale's own model might be termed the "submergence" model. He argues that professional socialization (in the army) for discipline, rationality, esprit de corps, the application of universalistic impersonal norms and reflexive (and not reflective) action only submerges primordial identities, which remain pertinent selectively in certain social fields. For instance, on the battlefield the tendency would be for these norms to hold — he cites as evidence that the Syrian army performed well in the 1973 war with Israel, whereas, for instance, in factional competition within the army, ethnicity might prevail. He argues that identities and roles are situationally specific, and the modernized roles and ethnic roles can be complementary and even mutually reinforcing: in a village or in the process of the contraction of marriage, sectarian norms might prevail, whereas in schools/barracks universalistic norms might prevail, and the disparate application of norms would be reinforced over time. Of course, all army officers are not just that but also fathers, villagers, tribesmen, sectmates, kinsmen, and Ba'thists, and the combination of applied norms differs in quite different situations. Moreover, the blend and weight of the complementarity (of ethnic and modernized roles) can differ from person to person and through time (the awareness of ethnicity in the Ba'th party was not in 1950 what it was in 1963, and not in 1963 what it is in 1989). Finally, Drysdale argues that the modernized model becomes less applicable and the ethnic or patrimonial model more applicable when professionalism is eroded by uncertainty: by political purges, factionalization of the officer corps, repeated intervention from on high in the promotion process, or the rapid promotion of "politically dependable" officers.

Although the insights of Battatu, Drysdale, Hinnebusch, and Sadowski are helpful in refining descriptive terms for various aspects of Syrian society and in questioning the applicability of various models for the study of that society, it is Fuad Khuri's new book that provides the most detailed and comprehensive model for resolving many of the ambiguities and complexities alluded to above.[22] For Khuri, the description and analysis of Middle Eastern society is best approached at a multi-institutional civilizational level, taking into account interlocking demographic, geographic, spatial, economic, and political factors. These factors are viewed as constraining and shaping religion, culture, and social organization in a feedback loop that emphasizes the density of symbols and signs, and the importance of popular religious ideology. Differences of religion and worldview constrain the structure of religious advancement (e.g., in the career profiles of Sunni vs. Shi'a *Ithna 'Ashariyya* religious specialists), the mode of political competition between and within elites, and the relationship of religious to state elites. Khuri's key contrasting social forms are "sect," "state," and "minority." The sects include the Druze, 'Ibadis, Zaydis, *Ithna 'Ashariyya*, Maronites, Yazidis and, most important for our purposes, Alawis. The sects contrast with the minorities (Copts, Greek Orthodox, Jews, Ismailis) who are dispersed in the polity and generally live in cities under the protection of the government on the one hand, and the state and the established religion (Sunni Islam) on the other. The sects are identified by a whole range of distinctive attributes including peripheral location, historical rebellion or dissimulation, demographic clustering in a territorial "homeland," a totalistic, stratified worldview, and exclusivity in culture and social organization including matters such as succession to office, spatial segregation, marriage, patron-client ties, law, personal names, and food.[23]

How does this model help to illuminate contemporary Syrian society? It does so by placing social categories and groups like the Alawis in a much wider societal context. The terms "Alawi" or "Shi'a" or "Maronite" refer not simply to an ethnic identity or a religious ideology, but also to a territory, a politico-economic system, a wide-ranging cultural repertoire, and a history. Although each sect reflects common attributes vis-à-vis the established religion and the state, and in contradistinction to the minorities, each sect also represents a unique blend of ideological, social organizational, and ritual attributes. Khuri argues that the differences of religious ideology are reflected in the social organization of religious specialists. The Alawis, rather than believing that God can be known through regular worship and indirectly through formal ritual specialists, hold that God can be known mysteriously but directly through "gates" (the *abwab*), that every age has living channels to the concealed pure religion (see Khuri, this volume). These "gates" stand at the top of an informal hierarchy of "religious sheikhs" (*shaykh al-din*) who possess esoteric, sacramental, religious knowledge. It is these religious sheikhs, rather than the "law sheikhs" (*shaykh al-shari'a*), who preside in the state religious courts, who are the focus of Alawite religion, of spiritual power, and who shape religious social organization (religious clientage).

Khuri stresses that in the sects religion is a pervasive influence in daily interaction reflected in oaths, contracts, witnessing, visiting sheikhs' tombs, and recitation of the biographies and proverbs of the most pious believers. Sect members participate in society at large and work in everyday occupations widespread in the polity. But they dichotomize their lives, all members feeling they are living in a special (religious) world valuable in itself and distinguished from all others.[24]

Khuri points out that besides the density of religious signs, symbols, and expressions in everyday life, and the proliferation of religious specialists with multiplex[25] roles in society at large, "sectarian" social organization and culture is characterized by dual religious organization. This dual religious organization contrasts with the religious organization of established religion, that of the Sunni Muslims. The Sunnis, according to Khuri, were the one religious category able to develop an organization suitable to accommodating state organization since, historically, in most countries of the Arab world they were the ruling elite who developed a centralized state system in the context of societies whose populations were relatively dense and stable. Since they were the ruling elite and they shaped state organization in their societies, the two hierarchies, governmental and religious, were merged with the category of religious scholars, *'ulema,* having second rank.

By contrast, the sects maintained a balanced, dual worldview and organization (as between state and religious leadership) with three subtypes: a relationship of antagonism and conflict (Zaydis and 'Ibadis); a blended dualism (Yazidis); and a relationship of complementary separation (Alawis, Druze, and Maronites). It is not possible to examine these subtypes in detail here, except to say that it is well known that there has been continuous conflict in both Yemen and Oman between leadership based on religious law (the rule of the imam), leadership based on tribal leaders (*shaykh*), and sporadically a tribal despot (sultan).

The Alawis, on the other hand, like the Druze and Maronites, ideologically define religion and polity as unitary but separate functionally. That is, the "religious sheikhs," the keepers and disseminators of esoteric religious knowledge, are separate from the mundane hierarchy of competing tribal, clan, and subsect coalitions (see Khuri, this volume). But there is a grafting and overlapping at the top level between mundane and religious leadership precisely because, ideologically, there is no separation of religious institution and state, and, as Khuri has astutely observed, the supreme leader of the sect takes on at once attributes of the imam and the hero. Khuri's conclusion is most important for all who wish to understand political life in contemporary Syrian society, and the role of religion and ethnicity within it: "Whoever emerges as a strong, unmatchable leader defending Alawi rights, consolidating their power and unity, maintaining cohesion and solidarity, is given a religious meaning, and becomes a historic symbol" (Khuri, this volume).

There is one other clear implication of Khuri's analysis for the role of Alawis in contemporary Syrian life. It has often been repeated that the Alawis represent a small minority of the Syrian population, one that emerged as dominant in government and polity as a result of its control of the army. However, the key to Alawi power and influence may be more their organization as a sect with certain territorial, demographic, ideological, spatial, and historical attributes that both allow and constrain a sectarian unity even in the presence of intrasectarian tribal and factional divisions. It is the same "religious sheikhs" who achieve prominence by their progressive withdrawal from society, including political affairs, for the pursuit of religious knowledge, and who practice austerity and monasticism, who also serve as the points of unity in a factionalized ethnic group.

It is not the purpose of this brief interpretive essay to do justice to Battatu's, Drysdale's, Sadowski's, and particularly Khuri's analyses. However, if the essay has succeeded in awakening the reader to the importance of exploring ethnicity, patrimonialism, and class in Syria, on the one hand in wider spatial and historical contexts, and on the other exploring them with a more detailed focus on religious ideology and culture, and their intimate ties to political structure and process, it will have served a secondary but nevertheless useful purpose.

ONE

Syrian Political Culture: A Historical Perspective

Philip S. Khoury

Political culture in Syria, indeed throughout the Fertile Crescent, did not change abruptly with the break up of the Ottoman Empire and the imposition of European rule after World War I. Rather, the exercise of political power followed the Ottoman model for thirty or more years after the collapse of the empire. It was only after World War II that this continuity was broken.

In order to support this contention, three periods of modern Syrian history, stretching from the mid-nineteenth century until the 1960s, need to be examined. Because the formation of political culture in Syria was intimately linked to the formation of a single elite in the nineteenth and early twentieth centuries, first it will be necessary to explain how this elite emerged and the character of its political role. This should tell us something about the foundations of politics in Syria. Then I will discuss the continuity of the elite's political role after the collapse of the Ottoman Empire — that is, between the two world wars, when Syria was ruled by the French. Finally, I will suggest the process by which this elite lost power after World War II, in the era of Syrian independence, and how and why political culture began to assume new forms and dimensions.

There always have been striking similarities between political developments in Syria and in the neighboring Arab regions. Political culture in the last century was shaped by a mixture of Ottoman administrative practices, local Arab traditions, and European intellectual and material influences. It was urban and rooted most deeply in the larger provincial cities of Syria, Lebanon, Palestine, and Iraq. In Syria's case, independent rural politics on anything more than a local scale was a phenomenon of the post–World War II era, when rural peoples, and especially the compact minorities, began their entrance onto the wider stage of national politics.

The political configuration of the larger Syrian cities during the Ottoman period suggests two areas of political power: one was external in the guise of the Ottoman state, and included the governor and imperial troops; the other was internal, filled by local groups possessing varying degrees of independent social and political influence, who acted as intermediaries between the state and the urban populace. The governors sent out from Istanbul often were not familiar with the Arabic language and local customs, and usually did not have sufficient military backing to exercise direct control in the provinces. To fill these gaps in their local knowledge and experience, governors had to rely on those local forces in the great cities that had independent influence in society. Their dependence allowed a particular type of politics to emerge in the Arab provinces: we call it, after Albert Hourani, a "politics of notables," and in some important ways we can see this mode of politics operating in Middle Eastern urban society as far back as the later Middle Ages.[1]

According to Hourani, where notables were most alike was in their aims: "to acquire leadership over the active forces of society — the craftsmen, the urban mobs, the popular religious leaders, the lords of the hill-valleys and the chiefs of Kurd, Turcoman, or Arab tribes; to eliminate or neutralise rival claimants to leadership; and to obtain influence with the Ottoman Governor."[2] But urban political position was not a passive status based on birth, wealth, and style. Political survival required a delicate balancing act. Local leaders could not appear to oppose the interests of the government, because they risked being deprived of their access to the ruler; nor could they jeopardize the interests of their local clientele, because they risked losing their independent influence and thus their usefulness to the ruler.

It was usual for local leaders to defend the social and political order by supporting the government. But there were occasions when they led movements against the government by mobilizing those popular forces from which they derived their independent influence. Such occasions arose when a particularly strong governor sought to dissolve the partnership between himself and the local notables, or when a weak governor no longer could maintain the stability that ensured the prosperity of the local leadership. Rarely, however, did urban leaders aim to overthrow the system of rule. Rather, their actions usually were intended to maintain the delicate balance between government and society. The important point to emphasize is that the various political and social movements, revolts, and urban insurrections that punctuated Syrian history in the nineteenth century were not at all revolutionary movements, but rather restorative movements.

Before the second half of the nineteenth century, notables may have had similar political aims, but they did not form a single sociological type; their social origins varied and this meant that the sources of their power did too.[3] There were the leaders of the great religious families, members of the *'ulemā* and the *ashraf*, the guardians of urban civilization and Islamic high culture. The religious families were mainly concentrated in the ancient quarters of the old walled city, near the cathedral mosque and central bazaar, where they had strong ties to the traditional commercial activities of production and trade. By the later Middle Ages, the great religious families were often the most prominent commercial families, so their wealth not only came from their control of pious trusts (*awqaf*), but also from their control of production and trade, and, by the eighteenth century, from hereditary tax farms around the cities.

The other group with independent influence were the commanders or chiefs of the local Janissary garrisons who had become lodged on a permanent basis in the cities by the eighteenth century. They are known as the *aghas*. By contrast to the *'ulemā* and the *ashraf*, the military chiefs and their supporters resided outside the city walls in what were really suburbs. The Maydan quarter to the south of the old town of Damascus is the most important suburb of this kind.[4] Bab al-Nayrab in Aleppo is the Maydan equivalent. These suburbs were far less homogeneous than the inner-city quarters, filled with all varieties of immigrants: uprooted peasants, semisedentarized tribes in for the winter season, a variety of non-Arab ethnic groups, the undifferentiated poor — Louis Chevalier's *classes dangereuses*, none of which were especially welcome inside the city walls.[5]

Military leaders derived power in two ways: by protecting those elements who were not welcome inside the city walls, by integrating them into their paramilitary organizations, and by dominating the grain and livestock trade that was so vital to the survival of urban life. Military chiefs could even hold cities at ransom by controlling the supply of grain to the towns or by fixing grain prices. In such circumstances, there was bound to be tension between the city center and the suburbs.

The *aghas* were both feared and despised by the more cosmopolitan, religious establishment, who found them socially repugnant and their power dangerous. The historical record indicates that most of the time the religious leadership and the military chiefs were in conflict with one another, though occasionally they joined hands against the Ottoman governor, especially if he was unusually ruthless or weak. The religious and mercantile establishments in the city center were more committed to upholding the status quo than were the *aghas,* for they were the true possessing classes in urban society. Because they had the most to lose, urban revolt was not their preferred weapon. Rather, they employed whenever possible more subtle, delicate kinds of pressure to achieve their ends.

Around the mid-nineteenth century a group of factors combined to encourage these rival urban groups with independent social and political influence to merge into a fairly unified elite with a single class base. The class that was formed by this merger would dominate Syrian political life virtually unchallenged until World War II.

Factors that encouraged the merger were connected to the gradual integration of Syria into a European-dominated economy in the nineteenth century, especially after the 1850s, and to the great Ottoman reformation — the Tanizmat, which marched hand in hand with European expansion into the Middle East. One corollary of the Tanzimat — that is, of the Ottoman centralization of power—was the growth and modernization of the rationalized and secularized state bureaucracy. Another corollary was the modernization of the army. The new Ottoman army may have done poorly on the battlefield against the European powers, but it brought a much greater measure of control over the Arab provinces, including Syria.

For the religious establishment and the military chiefs in towns like Damascus and Aleppo to survive, they had to adapt to the changing political climate. They could no longer move as freely between government and society as they had. Istanbul still had need for these intermediaries, but only those who were willing to identify themselves with the reinvigorated state and its new policies. To achieve and retain local political influence, a notable now had to move into the modern government institutions being set up in the provinces. Never before had notables in the towns been obliged to identify their interests as closely with the Ottoman state, or to distance themselves as far from their base in local society.

But local power was not solely a function of acquiring high government office in the provinces. It also became a function of acquiring private property on a large scale. Around the mid-nineteenth century, there developed a much greater interest in land as a principal source of wealth. This interest had to do with the expansion of the frontiers of cultivation in Syria, the settlement of tribes on these lands, and the commercialization of agriculture.[6] At the same time, the impact of the European industrial revolution had meant a gradual drying up of many traditional industries in the towns and of regional trade in local manufactures. Wealthy merchants began to turn to land as a more secure investment, and they wanted to own it outright. In response to these economic forces, the Ottoman state created the legal framework for the establishment of private property rights — rights that the state now institutionalized in new land laws.[7] Istanbul was conscious of the forces of change around the empire; it realized that it could not halt the spread of private property relations, but it could regularize its tax collection system on the land. Deeded private property meant more efficiently taxed property, and increased tax revenues could help pay for Ottoman modernization schemes.

If an urban notable happened to be in the right position in provincial government and knew how to use the new legal system, he and his family were in a most advantageous position to grab a large piece of real estate. By the 1870s, landownership and political power had begun to march hand in hand and would continue to do so until the 1950s, as it did in so much of the Middle East.

How was this merger between the religious-mercantile establishment and the *aghas* sealed? It so happens that the great families of the city center, who were so closely tied to the religious institutions, found it more difficult to break with the past and move into the modernized bureaucracy. In fact, they were quite defensive about all these changes. By contrast, the military chiefs-cum-grain merchants had less of a stake in the old order. Powerless to resist a reinvigorated Ottoman state, they moved into the administration more decisively. But in towns like Damascus and Aleppo, the great urban families of the city center possessed one thing that had always been desired by these social pariahs in the suburbs, the *aghas*: pedigree or social status. Intermarriage could bring benefits to both groups: social status to the *aghas* and easier access to government and to wealth through land to the religious families, who, incidentally, were beginning to experience a loss of influence as their monopoly of the legal and educational institutions decayed in the face of creeping secularization.

Just after the mid-nineteenth century, religious leaders broke with social custom by supporting marriages outside their network of families. By the turn of the twentieth century, both groups of city leaders had crystalized into a single elite with a similar economic base in land and political power in government office. A much more stable local upper class now existed in the large cities of Syria, as it did elsewhere in the Fertile Crescent.

Apart from landownership on a large scale and high government offices, this new class acquired other characteristics that helped to give it shape. It retained them long after the collapse of the Ottoman Empire. One characteristic was a distinctive Ottoman aristocratic behavior and style, which urban notables acquired as they were drawn more completely into the Ottoman system of rule. They took the new railroads to Istanbul for an Ottoman professional education in Turkish to prepare them to administer their provinces. They now spoke Turkish politely alongside Arabic. And they adopted the new Turkish upper-class dress— the frock coat and the fez. These Ottoman trappings widened the social gap between them and the rest of local Arab society. The schools in Istanbul, which the sons of the Syrian upper class attended, were generally public administration schools, not military academies. Because their fathers thought that military careers were beneath their dignity and social position, they used all kinds of connections to secure exemptions from military service for their sons. Syrian notables carried this hostile attitude toward military service with them into the twentieth century. It contributed to their own downfall after World War II.

The other characteristic that the notables also took with them into the twentieth century was an inclination to intense political factionalism. Their factionalism was not based so much on fictive or confessional alignments, but on rival, clan-based patronage alliances.

The question arises, however: If, by the turn of the twentieth century, the Syrian political elite belonged to the same class and retained similar methods, styles, and aims, why is it that its members felt no obligation to close ranks and clarify their common interests as a class on crucial political issues? Why were they so prone to factionalism? The answer lies in the reality that until World War II they faced no serious challenge from further down the social scale to the exclusive position that they had carved out for themselves at the summit of politics in Syria. It was only on the eve of World War II that the political elite began to sense a rising danger to its position from restless classes and forces further down in society. It is only after the war that this danger crystalized into organized movements to depose the veteran elite and break up the social bases of its power. Only then did the elite close ranks, but it was too late. Before the war, the Syrian upper class was (to use Marx's language) a "class in itself" but not a "class for itself."[8]

To sum up, by World War I, the major political movements in Syria were led by members of these same notable families who brought to them a certain style of political action and a common way of looking at the world, which they had acquired in late Ottoman times. The formation, consolidation, and continued influence of the local political elite were made possible by its greater access to government and to landownership.

But there was one more factor that allowed the elite to remain at the summit of local politics. This was its seizure, on the eve of World War I, of the ascendant ideology of Arab nationalism. Its identification with this new system of ideas helped it to preserve its monopoly over local politics for two more generations.

Where studies of the rise of Arab nationalism fall short is in their ne-
glect to explain how and why the idea of Arabism is translated into a full-
blown political movement. This has been the concern of a new generation
of historians of Arab nationalism, which is indebted to C. Ernest Dawn's
pioneering essays.[9]

A most convincing explanation for how and why this new idea of
Arab nationalism was activated before World War I is in terms of a conflict within the Syrian urban elite, whether in Damascus and Aleppo, Beirut and Tripoli, or Jerusalem and Jaffa. Arab nationalism arose as an opposition movement around 1900 and accelerated after 1908, once the
Ottoman Committee of Union and Progress began to enforce administrative centralization, streamline the provincial bureaucracy, and install
Turks in a number of critical posts. A growing number of Syrian notables
lost their positions in the Ottoman system, and it was they who first
turned the idea of Arabism into a vehicle for expressing their grievances
with Istanbul and for regaining their positions. By contrast, many notables who managed to hold on to their posts in the provinces stood by the
empire until its collapse in 1918. Such an analysis has a certain Weberian
ring to it: the bureaucratic "haves" vs. the "have-nots."[10]

There is disagreement among historians as to the extent of Arab nationalism's appeal before 1918. Some argue that the Arab opposition
movement appealed to only a minority of politically conscious elites in
greater Syria before 1918, others that by 1914 Arab nationalists had already become a majority.[11] But there is general agreement that the resentment of extreme Young Turk centralization policies (some also add
Zionism) obliged local Arab elites to abandon Ottomanism, the reigning
ideology of the empire, for Arabism.[12]

The point to underscore is that by World War I, Arabism had become
the ascendant idea and movement of the times in Syria. During the war,
when many notables began to jump from the sinking Ottoman ship, they
grabbed, as they fell, the rope of Arab nationalism. They really had no
other choice. It was this rope that enabled them to swing into the interwar
years with their political and social influence intact.

For the most part, men important in local affairs under the Ottomans
were the same men, or their sons, who wielded political influence under
the French. Political leaders organized their personal support systems in
interwar Syria as they had in Ottoman Syria. In Ottoman times, political
power was based in the city and then extended from there to the settled
countryside and eventually into the seminomadic areas. Under the

French, political power likewise emanated from the city. Moreover, the methods that urban leaders used to acquire political power and their aims remained constant. Whatever the projected scope of power and whoever the political overlord, the basic building block of political influence in Syria was the same: urban leadership.

The new system devised to replace Ottoman rule was, of course, the Mandate system.[13] And though in principle the Mandate system never was intended to be a traditional system of European colonial rule, in fact the way the French administered Syria after the war, and the policies they pursued, had many important features in common with prewar French colonialism.

Like any formal colony, Syria was expected to pay its own way financially. It had to foot the bill for the French army of occupation and the French administration. A rather typical system of colonial finance was imposed on the Syrians. Revenues came from indirect taxes, especially customs revenues. And a high proportion of government expenditure was on security and defense, not on agriculture, industry, health, or education. Although according to the League of Nations the French were to be granted no special privileges in Syria, in practice they disregarded this. To complicate matters, the Syrian currency was pegged to the French franc, and for the Syrian people this meant untold misery in the 1920s and again in the late 1930s, because of the franc's wide fluctuations. Syrians on a fixed income suffered most in these circumstances, in particular intellectuals and bureaucrats—groups that could cause a foreign power all kinds of headaches when provoked.

But the Mandate system was never a direct system of rule. The French, like the Turks before them, needed a partner in order to govern. For one thing, the League of Nations obliged the mandatory power to prepare the Syrian people for independence; for another, France's postwar economy was so fragile that it could no longer afford direct rule abroad. Nonetheless, there was a significant difference in the nature of the new imperial authority: it was illegitimate and thus was unstable. France was not recognized to be a legitimate overlord, as the sultan-caliph of the Ottoman Empire had been. The Turks had behind them four centuries of rule and the very important component of a common religious tradition.[14] France had the dubious, even in Western eyes, legitimization conferred by the weak and imperfectly conceived Mandate system. Because France historically had tried to establish and strengthen its position in the Levant by posing as the protector of the Christians, it was doubly distrusted by the Muslim majority of the region. In part because it was considered illegitimate and in part because of certain exogenous factors —

the international and moral restrictions of the Mandate system and the fragility of France's postwar economic and political order—its position in Syria was inherently unstable, much more so than the Ottoman position ever had been.

Contributing to this instability of rule was the reality that the French did not have the resources to buy loyalty on a large scale or to develop the Syrian economy either for the Syrians or for themselves. To start with, Syria was not inherently resource-rich. Oil discoveries were insignificant and cotton production faced a serious setback with the development of synthetics in France and elsewhere. French monetary policies had disastrous financial repercussions. The devastation wrought by World War I, the debilitating reorientation forced on the Syrian economy by the partition of geographical Syria and the creation of distinct and separate mandatory regimes, and the continued erosion of Syrian industry by the spread of the European economy helped to create and maintain high unemployment and inflation, all of which added to the political instability inherent in the Mandate situation.[15] Then, there were specific French policies that inflamed traditional sectarian conflict by distinctly favoring minorities and by promoting a series of administratively isolated minority enclaves. The French threatened the Muslim majority by seizing control of their institutions and debasing the symbols of their culture.

Above all, France ruled Syria with eyes on the French empire in North Africa; it was not a focus that helped make a sound policy in Syria. Not only was every act of policy in Syria judged by its possible effects on North Africa, but the very categories by which Syria was understood were drawn from French experience in North Africa. And these categories simply did not fit the Syrian situation. Syria was not Morocco. The French could not impose stability by playing the minorities against the Sunni Muslim majority, the countryside against the cities, and the nationalist factions against one another.[16]

The French saw Arab nationalism as a force that had to be eliminated before it spread to North Africa and infected the very heart of the French empire. They actually thought they could destroy Arab nationalism outright. The British were different. They did not invent Arab nationalism (as the French thought or as some unsympathetic historians have argued), but they knew early on that it was a force that would not wither away quietly on a sandy Mediterranean beach. Nor did they think they could crush it outright. What they could do, however, was try to cultivate it, and especially its more moderate leaders. They could build these leaders up, tie their interests to British interests, and then have them contain (with discreet British encouragement) the more radical forces in the nationalist movement. Their technique was particularly successful in Iraq, although not in Palestine. By the time the French understood its advantages, it was already too late.

How did these changes in the balance between French rule and local leadership condition Syrian nationalist political behavior in the interwar years? They did not force the notables to vary their major aims much from what they were in late Ottoman times. The notables — now grouped into an array of nationalist organizations and connected from town to town — still sought to rally the active forces of Syrian society behind their respective bloc or party; they still aimed to neutralize all local rivals; and they still wanted to appear as the sole figures of influence with whom the French would have to cooperate to govern Syria.

To a certain extent politics changed with the imposition of European rule, but it still operated within the old Ottoman framework. The difference was that Syrian urban leadership was obliged to create a new balance of power between itself and the French. The French, like the Ottomans before them, had to govern in association with elements from the urban upper classes. But given the intrinsic illegitimacy of France's position and its penchant for dictatorial policy without regard for the position and interests of the local elite, many urban leaders became forces of opposition. They had to appear more as the spokesmen of the people in the halls of power than as agents of the French. To gain recognition from this strong-minded regime, they not only had to mobilize the popular forces in society, but they also had to seek broader political alliances than before between the different cities and regions, between the Sunni Muslim majority and the religious and ethnic minorities, and between themselves and like-minded elites in the neighboring Arab territories. Hence they required not only a shared dedication of purpose, but an ideology to express this new solidarity and drive. Nationalism provided the kind of ideological cohesion and emotional appeal that urban leaders needed to be politically effective between the wars.

How did urban leaders shape nationalism into an instrument by which to create a more desirable balance between themselves and the French? They molded their movement to suit the particular interests of their class. In their hands, nationalism never was a revolutionary idea with profound social content; rather it was an instrument to win French recognition without upsetting the status quo. Nationalism remained a simplistic idea: in its romanticized vision of the Arab past, it appealed to the hearts and minds of a broad section of Arab society. It was an attractive and compelling ideology, more so because it was able to capitalize on Islam's political misfortunes by absorbing the important component of religious solidarity. The very language of this brand of nationalism indicated its class foundations. Apart from the aim of independence, nationalism incorporated the liberal bourgeois language of constitutionalism, parliamentary forms, and personal freedoms. But hardly a word was heard about economic and social justice. This was the last thing the nationalist landowners — still able to collect their generous rents from the ground — were interested in discussing.

In a rather closed political system like the Syrian, where one broad class was organized into a set of rival clan-based alliances and was fairly free of pressures from below, parliament was an ideal, genteel place in which factions could play out their struggles and ambitions. The nationalist elite simply adored parliamentary life and nothing caused them to complain louder than when the French suspended parliament, as they so often did between the wars.

Local politics was played out in the Syrian towns in a situation where patronage systems cut through and deflected horizontal, class-based politics.[17] For much of the interwar era, nationalist leaders concentrated on mobilizing merchants, popular religious leaders, quarter bosses, and the urban mob on an intermittent basis against the Mandate authorities. However, the character of patronage also began to change in the 1930s, in both class and spatial terms. The base of the nationalist movement gradually shifted away from the popular classes in the old quarters where religious chiefs and local gang leaders had traditionally mobilized the street; it shifted toward the new institutions such as the modern secondary schools, the university, the modern professional societies of lawyers, doctors, and engineers, the infant trade unions,[18] and the emerging youth organizations and sporting clubs, all of which were lodged in the newer, modern districts of the cities. Although this transition was by no means complete at the end of the Mandate, by the late 1930s it was clearly irreversible.

For the political leadership, nationalism was certainly a useful instrument by which to mobilize forces so as to convince the French to bargain with them. But it also had the potential to completely alienate the French and thus destroy the delicate balance between French rule and the nationalists.

So when the local leadership appealed to nationalism and behind that to religious solidarity, they had to temper this appeal by acts of "political prudence."[19] In fact, nationalists much preferred to mobilize urban forces only on a temporary basis — that is, when these forces could be useful to the elite's specific short-term aims. Mass mobilization on anything like a permanent basis was something to be avoided at all costs. At times, the elite feared mobilizing the streets, the mosques, and the school yards even more than they feared the French. For mass mobilization could turn ugly—it could backfire in the face of the elite nationalist leadership. For decades, the absentee landowning class and its politically active members had worked within a delicate but comfortable framework in which they played out their factional politics; they rightly feared that politics might break out of that framework.

It did break out for nearly two years during the Great Revolt of 1925–1927, the most significant rebellion of the 1920s in the Arab world. This genuinely popular uprising among the Druze minority that spread to Damascus and beyond, obliged nationalists to throw their weight behind the rebellion in order to hold on to their leadership. Although the Syrian political leadership adopted the language of revolution and even some revolutionary tactics during this period, it did so reluctantly, after more subtle and delicate diplomatic efforts to bring about some relaxation of foreign control had failed. And while their methods may have seemed revolutionary, their aims were really restorative, not transformatory.[20]

After two years the revolt collapsed in the face of a reinforced French army of occupation, leaving the nationalist leadership in a much weakened state. Although nationalists were relieved to drop armed confrontation as a strategy for winning French recognition, their future now hinged on French receptivity. Fortunately, the revolt's fierceness and duration had also convinced the French of the need to make some concession to the desire of self-government in Syria. A constitution was promulgated in 1930 and a parliament elected in 1932. This was an unforeseen break for a defeated and demoralized nationalist leadership; it gave it a new lease on life. It was now able to adopt the more familiar and comfortable tactics of intermittent protest mixed with diplomacy in an effort to restore the type of balance between foreign rule and local leadership that had been operative in late Ottoman times.

And so when Syria did achieve independence, it was not by popular struggle or revolt, but by intermittent protest coupled with diplomatic activity. This could be seen in 1936 when the nationalist leadership conducted a fifty-day general strike after years of unsuccessfully trying to advance their aims of unity and independence. The strike was immediately followed by diplomacy in Paris, which finally brought the nationalists into government for the first time and into a power-sharing relationship with the French. And it could be seen again even more vividly during World War II when nationalists conducted largely nonviolent strikes and demonstrations, while they built a new set of delicate relationships, in this case with a third party, Britain, which had come to hold the balance of power in Syria during the war. This is just the way the nationalists wanted to achieve independence. Their methods did not upset the status quo, and they enabled the veteran nationalists to take control of government after the French were obliged to withdraw from Syria at the end of the war.[21]

Albert Hourani has suggested that with independence the conditions for the old kind of political expertise in Syria disappeared. The most obvious change was that, for the first time, the veteran nationalists no longer could put themselves forward as brokers between the Ottoman state and Arab society or as popular leaders in the face of an alien authority like the French, but as the rulers of their own country. For the first time, they were in a position to use the state apparatus as a means of coercion. They did not need a partner or intermediary, or want one. Basically, the age of a "politics of notables" gave way to a new age and a different type of politics.[22]

But the old framework did not give way suddenly. The urban, absentee landowning class and the leadership it produced did not immediately dissolve after generations of activity. They held on for nearly twenty years after independence, longer than their counterparts in Egypt and Iraq.

Still, from their first day in the driver's seat in Damascus, their prospects were bleak. Already, they were faced with a rising danger from those restless forces further down the social scale that had first begun to organize in the 1930s but were unable to break out of the old framework of clan-based factions as long as the French remained in the country. It was these new forces, of course, that eventually brought an end to the old way of politics. Indeed, it might be argued that they brought an end to "politics" altogether in Syria.

In any case, with independence, something had changed. Profound structural changes in economy and society, which had begun during the world depression and had accelerated during World War II, unleashed new forces with new methods and aims, which weakened the old framework. The politics of notables was replaced by a politics of bureaucracies, but also by a politics of regionalism, and more precisely by a politics of the countryside, of rural forces struggling against more established urban elements for control of the cities and of government.

Hanna Batatu has described a familiar pattern:

> rural people, driven by economic distress or lack of security, move into the main cities, settle in the outlying districts, enter before long into relations or forge common links with elements of the urban poor, who are themselves often earlier migrants from the countryside, and together they challenge the old established

classes. [But,] in sharp contrast to the outcome of urban-rural conflicts of past centuries, the country people clinched a more enduring, if unstable, victory by virtue of their deep penetration of the Syrian army.[23]

The veteran elite had snubbed that army for so long.

The urban leadership lost power in Syria because it failed to wed nationalism to state power. Hourani has written:

> new political ideas — radical nationalism, social reform, and Islamic assertion — provided the channels through which other social groups could pursue their interests: the growing middle class of the cities, teachers and students, and the army officers, many of them of rural origin and destined in the end to destroy the basis of the social power of the old elite, their control of the land.[24]

Beyond this, these new forces demanded the right to open up and take an active part in the political process, previously closed to them.

The veteran leadership eventually found it impossible to exclude the newly radicalized intelligentsia and elements from the compact minorities — Druzes, Ismailis, and especially Alawis — who came from peasant or lower middle-class origin, and from the rural hinterland or smaller towns. Nothing could prevent them from redefining their relations with one another or with the veteran elite in government. On the political level, these new forces gravitated toward modern political organizations — the communists, the Muslim Brethren, and the Ba'th Party, which had begun to make their ascent in the years prior to independence.[25]

With their more rigorous systems of ideas and their more sophisticated methods of organization, they criticized and challenged the veteran elite in several concrete ways: for failing to uphold the reigning idea of pan-Arab unity; for contributing to the Arab failure to save Palestine in 1948; and for retaining strong, compromising ties to the ex-colonial power.[26] This same pattern could be detected in Egypt and Iraq. These radicalized forces shifted the emphasis of nationalism to better accommodate the accelerated changes taking place in economy and society. The language of nationalism no longer emphasized constitutionalism, parliamentary forms, or personal freedoms, but rather social and economic justice for the masses, neutralism in international politics, and, in the case of the eventually triumphant Ba'th Party, pan-Arab unity. Nationalism stressed mass education, land reform, social welfare, and rapid industrialization, all of which were to be brought about by a strong, dynamic, interventionist state, all for the good of the masses. Government was to be "for the people, but not by the people."

To quote Hourani again:

In this new age, the political struggle takes place on two levels. Those inside the system of government compete for favoured access to the ruler and control of important positions of power in the administration. Those outside must aim at a total overthrow of the government, using the only method which seems likely to be effective: the armed forces.[27]

Who got control of the army, of course, were the rural folk—members of the compact minorities—in particular, the Alawis, a dispossessed mountain and hill community armed with a strange heterodox brand of Islam, who were fiercely tribal. The French had encouraged them to join the army during the Mandate. More importantly, they saw the military as their one avenue for social advancement, beyond the squalor and isolation in which they lived.

Once the Alawis began to penetrate the military in significant numbers, they used their rural, regional, tribal, and religious solidarity to monopolize its levers of command. At first, they aligned with rural Sunnis in the armed forces to weaken urban Sunnis who were in control of the army immediately after independence. Then, the Alawis turned on their rural Sunni allies and the smaller minority communities like the Druzes in the army.[28] And finally the Alawis fought out their own internal wars, with the cleverest faction winning out in the end, the one headed by Hafiz al-Asad.

That elements among the veteran elite managed to retain influence in politics as late as the early 1960s suggests just how tenacious and resilient they were in the face of the growing forces of radicalization in the military and in civilian society. But in the end, they were swept aside rather easily. And with their departure, an old way of political life disappeared in Syria.

Today there are fewer and fewer reminders of the time when Syrian political culture and urban notables were so closely identified with one another. For the historian, perhaps the most vivid reminder of that age is the Azm Palace in the Suq Saruja quarter of Damascus, which is both a museum and the home of the national historical archives. There, the historian can examine a partial but illuminating record of the achievements and failings of Syria's urban notables in some of the very rooms in which they hatched their political undertakings. What better way to reconstruct the past.

Two

Class and State in Ba'thist Syria

Raymond A. Hinnebusch

This essay explores the role of class in Syria's politics and the effect of state policy under the Ba'th on its class structure. Some deny the relevance of class, viewing small groups, particularly sects, as the effective units of Syrian politics.[1] This is attributed to a mosaic society and particularistic culture, or an authoritarian state intolerant of open politics. Some, too, dismiss the effect of state action on the class structure, viewing the class ideologies of radical elites as mere facades for power struggles.[2]

It is impossible to make sense of modern Syrian political development without resort to the class variable. This is not to dispute the importance of group politics in a mosaic society and kinship culture in which sect and family were the inherited "natural" units of political action. However, after a century of capitalist penetration and modernization, Syria is no longer a simple segmental society but a complex one in which "vertical" units coexist with classes. Political action has not typically taken the form of large class formations in open conflict. But the political conflicts of greatest consequence, those that have driven systemic change, have pitted coalitions, which, though heterogeneous (often including sectarian and occupation groups), were brought together by class interests in battles over class-related issues, such as the distribution of wealth arising from a certain mode of production and relations to the world capitalist centers.

No claim is made that the state is always an instrument of class power, for it may be an arena of conflict or autonomous of classes, but class origins have powerfully shaped the ideology of political elites and there have been periods when the state has been used as an instrument of class defense or, particularly under the radical Ba'th, of "revolution from above," against the dominant classes. Such radical periods are typically temporary and to the very extent they break down class cleavages and increase individual or group mobility, class alignments often give way to other ways of organizing the political arena; indeed, this happened under Asad. But the consolidation of Asad's state cannot be understood except as an outcome of the class transformations of the 1960s. This is to argue that, in Syria as elsewhere, class structure shapes the type and nature of the state and hence the very character of politics.

This chapter cannot pretend to marshal the evidence needed to prove the case for class, but a survey of certain watersheds in the development of state and class, addressing the role and importance of class in each and considering conflicting interpretations, particularly the role of sect, will illustrate the argument. By way of showing how little Syrian politics is unique or immune from the class politics found in the West, parallels will be drawn with France, whose history is often taken to manifest most clearly the relation of state and class.

Class Structure, Class Conflict, and Political Mobilization under the Ancien Régime: The Origins of the Ba'thist Party

The rise of the Ba'thist Party cannot be understood apart from the class structure of traditional Syria, because the impact of social change on this structure generated the forces — new classes and class alliances — and the grievances, at base rooted in class inequalities, which led to the fall of the ancien régime. Essentially, the rise of the Ba'thists and the fall of the old regime were a product of two dovetailing developments: a conflict of lord and peasant, and the rise of a salaried new middle class challenging the landlord regime.

Syria's landlord-peasant cleavage was rooted in the nineteenth century penetration of capitalism which gave rise to great landed estates at the expense of the peasants. An urban-based landed class, separated from the peasantry by a great cultural gap and lacking major political and economic functions in the village, was thereby created. This development was never legitimized in peasant eyes. A highly inegalitarian agrarian social structure resulted: two thirds of the peasants were turned into semi-servile sharecroppers on the great latifundia, but even small-holding peasants were in the grip of merchants and moneylenders. Monopolistic ownership of land and control of markets defined a system of productive relations by which the city lived off a surplus extracted from peasants.

The state was erected directly on this social base: control of land and markets translated into dependency and clientalism, supporting a political elite made up almost exclusively of the landed notables. This was a clear case of class rule: the state was indeed little more than the executive committee of the landed-commercial ruling class.[3]

Capitalist penetration and state formation—the creation of a modern bureaucracy, army and education system — set in motion economic growth and social-mobilization which undermined this traditional order. These forces gave rise to a salaried new middle class, a significant element of which was recruited from the village; but social mobilization outstripped economic development, frustrating the aspirations of this new class and, when the capitalist boom was exhausted and the economy turned down in the mid-fifties, middle class alienation spread widely. Capitalist penetration also eroded clientalist ties and set off a proletarianization of the peasantry; thus the condition of the peasants and their ties to the old order simultaneously declined, leaving many "available" for antisystem mobilization.

This social change, in fact, precipitated a political mobilization, and, in time, the formation of a middle-class, peasant coalition against the old regime based on demands for land reform and "socialism"—that is, populist redistribution of opportunity and a leading role for the state in the economy. Middle class and peasant also shared a common radical nationalism, pan-Arab and anti-imperialist, born and fueled by the Palestine disaster and subsequent Western and Israeli pressures on Syria, to which the old elite, linked to the West, offered no effectual response. The key link between middle class and peasantry was the rural intelligentsia, a pivotal political force that bridged the urban-rural gap and shared the grievances of both classes against the landed elite. Once the expansion of the armed forces opened the military academy to this element, the ruralization and plebianization of the officer corps made it a hotbed of nationalist and populist agitation, and the striking force that would eventually bring down the old regime.[4]

Minority groups, notably Alawis and Druze, played a central role in the rural intelligentsia and in the officer corps. But this does not make the conflict of the 1950s sectarian. Rather, these elements are best seen as the vanguard of the middle-class peasant alliance. Classes almost always mobilize *unevenly,* with some regions and segments affected earlier than others. That was so of Syria's peasantry, for very specific reasons. The mountain peasantry, having escaped direct control by the landlords of the plains, retained more independence and gained earlier access to education than most other villagers. Yet, under severe population pressure on meager land resources and threatened by landlord-merchant encroachment, peasant youth there were being pushed out of agriculture earlier than elsewhere. Fortuitously, opportunities in the army and as village school teachers also were opening up for them. The mountain peasantry tended to be minoritarian, since, historically, only there could minorities survive the pressure of Sunni orthodoxy. The minorities were also more rapidly politicized, partly from their early social mobilization but also because they carried a double grievance against the ancien régime, alienated on both class and sectarian grounds. This would make the Alawis, in particular, the most radical vanguard of the peasantry, the group that had the most to gain and least to lose from an overturning of the old regime. But they mobilized not as Alawis demanding sectarian relief or privilege, but as part of a broader movement linking them with other non-Alawi plebian elements making broader class demands—land reform for the entire poor peasantry.[5]

The Ba'thist Party became the main instrument through which the middle-class, peasant coalition was shaped. Its nationalist-populist/etatist ideology best expressed the common interests of the two classes. Its core, recruited from the rural intelligentsia, best incorporated the link of middle class and village. These two factors, in turn, enabled it to build a strong following in the military. The Ba'thists initially fostered this coalition, but gradually it became the vehicle of these wider social forces, sometimes against the wishes of its founding leaders.[6]

Yet the coalition the Ba'thists put together proved exceedingly vulnerable to fragmentation and it collapsed under the United Arab Republic and separatist regimes, leaving only several scattered segments. In particular, it lost many of its Sunni middle-class elements owing to splits with Nasir and the break off of Akram Hawrani's faction. This was a manifestation of the fragility of class alliances in a mosaic society where they must incorporate a wide diversity of sectarian and regional factions committed to different leaders and shades of ideology. Also at work was a problem unique to Syria's history as a state corresponding to no felt nation—that is, conflicting commitments to differing units of national-statehood, and the powerful appeal of pan-Arab unionism. But the rural core of the Ba'thist movement remained in being, and it was leading military elements of this core, which engineered the coup, toppling the old regime and bringing the Ba'thists to power. The Ba'thists therefore seized power by military coup, not at the head of a broad cross-class movement. But this should not disguise the fact that the coup represented a delayed outcome of the political mobilization of the 1950s, and expressed a "green uprising" against the traditional establishment.

The new Ba'thist leaders were products of the village, officers and intellectuals of rural origin from the mountain peasant minorities communities, and, to a lesser extent, mainstream Sunni peasantry and provincial towns. Their outlook — a combination of radical nationalism and populism — was shaped by these social roots and by the agrarian crisis and struggle against the notable elite of the 1950s. Their enemies were urban, chiefly the old landlord elite and Islamic conservatives in tenuous alliance with urban middle-class Nasserites and liberals. The Ba'th particular road to power, on the back of the army, lacking an organized mass base, would dictate the military and authoritarian character of the regime it would build. But it also enjoyed a potential, if scattered and demobilized, constituency in the village which it would set about remobilizing from above and which would become a key to regime consolidation.[7]

The forces behind the rise of the Ba'thists — imperialist intervention, agrarian crisis and peasant politicization, economic development and social mobilization, giving rise to a new class challenging the dominant one, followed by a developmental crisis — are the typical forces behind revolutions and radical movements everywhere. Although it clearly took place on a much lesser scale with far less mass mobilization, there are even certain parallels in the Syrian case with a "great revolution" like the French: the combination of middle-class radicalism — Jacobinism — and peasant discontent against a regime of landed power. The Ba'thists can be convincingly analyzed only in such terms. Had its rise been a function of mere sectarian rivalries or military praetorianism, it would have proven evanescent, instead of the most durable and successful of Syria's modern political movements.

The Ba'thist Revolution from Above: Radical Jacobism Takes Command (1963–1970)

The goal of the new Ba'thist leaders was not just another coup but a revolution. Indeed, the years after the coup bear all the telltale marks of "revolution from above."

1. A whole new political elite of a distinctly plebian, rural, lower middle-class, "ex-peasant" social composition was catapulted into state power, decisively displacing the traditional urban notable elite and, before long, the elder Ba'thist leaders from control of the party.[8]

2. The new regime developed a revolutionary doctrine, a radicalized version of Ba'thism, incorporating major elements of Marxism-Leninism. Notably, it decided to create a Leninist party-state to mobilize a mass base, and embraced the Marxist belief in the bankruptcy of the bourgeoisie and the capitalist road to development.[9]

3. This was rightly viewed as a declaration of class warfare by all sides in Syria, and it set off a three-sided power struggle over Syria's future — indeed, quite explicitly, over control of the means of production and the state.

a) One struggle pitted the Ba'thist regime against an urban-based opposition led by the *Ikhwan,* the merchants and the landed families, which spoke the language of free enterprise and conservative Islam. For a while, middle-class Nasserites made up another component of the opposition. It is quite true that the class character of this struggle was thus initially diluted by another issue — that of union with Egypt, which divided the salaried middle class, to a considerable extent on urban-rural and sectarian lines, with Nasserism strongest among urban Sunnis. But this hardly negates the fact that the dominant conflict of the 1963 – 1970 period was an intense struggle between class-shaped coalitions, expressed by rival class-shaped ideologies — Ba'thism and political Islam. The major axis of conflict pitted a patrician-led coalition defending the accumulated interests of a traditional urban society hitherto dominant over the village and a government in the hands of plebian elements animated by the profound hostility of both the small official and peasant toward "feudalists" and "middlemen."

b) A second struggle was played out inside the party itself in which the chief and most enduring distinction between the two sides was social origins and rival class-shaped interpretations of Ba'thism. The party moderates spoke for the urban middle class from which they came and sought a reformist road to development in which the state could secure the cooperation of capital, yet direct it into national development and widen social opportunities for the lesser strata. The radicals spoke for the provincial lower middle class and the peasants, who, much more hostile to the urban establishment, sought to demolish its power in a revolution from above. This struggle did take complicated forms. It sometimes appeared as a personal power rivalry with a certain civil-military dimension and it had a sectarian aspect. In the major showdown, a Sunni general, Amin Hafiz, championed the moderates and exploited Sunni resentment of minority dominance in the regime, while Salah Jedid, an Alawi officer, used minority fear of Sunni resentment to build a coalition behind the radicals. In a situation of power struggle and intense insecurity, rivals exploited every available tie and cleavage. Blocs naturally tended to form among those who, from the same region or sect, felt a greater degree of mutual trust. But this does not mean that political conflicts were mere struggles between regional or sectarian blocs. Rival coalitions were built of a multitude of ties and ultimately the blocs that crystalized on both sides were cross-sectarian, civil-military coalitions unified and distinguished chiefly by opposing ideologies. Sectarianism was not an end in itself, but a means to personal power or ideological ends.[10]

4. The radical regime transformed the class composition of the state. The Ba'thization of the army replaced Sunni upper-middle and middle-class officers by ones of plebian, rural, and often minority origin. The Alawi community was increasingly incorporated into the state, a recruitment that had double sectarian and class dimensions. Although in one respect Alawis acquired favored access to power, in another respect they played the role of a surrogate proletariat, the most radical contingent in the regime coalition, with the strongest stake in defending and advancing the revolution. But, in addition to this, the regime incorporated, through party and syndical organization, land reform and a challenge to local notables, a village base, an alliance of educated village youth and the small-holding peasantry. In the cities, sections of the radical intelligentsia, the state-dependent white-collar class, and militant trade-unionists were also won over to the ruling coalition. Thus, a regime with an initially narrow base was able to use national-populism to reach down to lower strata and peripheral areas, and outflank its rivals in the old urban center.[11]

5. The politices of the regime had a clear class bias, which distributed costs and benefits quite unequally, to the advantage of its plebian constituency and at the expense of the notables and the *suq*. Land reform, nationalizations, and government control over the market struck at the economic bases of the bourgeoisie—that is, their control of the means of production—land, factories—and of the market. These policies also sharply narrowed their political bases — rooted in dependence and patronage—outside the *suq*. This regime could very well be described as a "dictatorship of the petite bourgeoisie," if that is taken to mean one of the government-dependent salaried middle class and the small-holding peasantry. But the mercantile petite bourgeoisie was hostile to a regime constantly at war with the *suq*.

6. This policy of class struggle deliberately polarized society. In the aftermath of the 1967 war, however, Syria could no longer afford internal conflict and a wing of the Ba'thist Party under General Hafiz al-Asad demanded an end to this strategy in favor of its opposite: national unity. This set off another power struggle inside the Ba'thists, over Asad's proposal for détente with the bourgeoisie, both Syrian and Arab. A duality of power emerged in the regime, presenting a clear choice of radicalization or liberalization. The opposing sides were cross-sectarian and civil-military coalitions, but otherwise appealed to differing constituencies: Syria's bourgeoisie and the army high command preferred Asad, while leftist intellectuals, trade unionists, and peasant cadres backed the radicals. But with the main levers of military power in his hands by 1970,

Asad broke the stalemate, deposed the radicals in an intraparty coup, and took power himself.[12]

In Syria, as in postrevolutionary France, the revolutionary coalition split, with plebian "radicals" (Jacobins) seizing the initiative from more socially established and wavering "moderates," and entrenching the basics of the revolution before overextending themselves and opening the door to a conservative "Thermidor."

Social Leveling: The Social Structural Outcome of Ba'thist Reforms

The social structural consequences of the Ba'thist revolution from above were by no means inconsequential. First, the regime's social leveling — nationalizations and agrarian reform — demolished rigid class inequalities rooted in monopolistic control of the means of production and, more broadly, diffused property. Second, an enormous increase in the size and socio-economic role of the state—the army, bureaucracy, education system, and the large public sector, the main channel of investment in the economy—made it a major channel of upward mobility and an obstacle to a reconcentration of private control over the means of production. Together, these developments resulted in a more fluid social terrain. The private sector persisted, dominating much of commerce, construction, real estate, and small trade. Most land remained wholly or in practice private freehold. But the leveling of the top, the rise of the state, and the dispersion of property certainly expressed the interests of the regime's coalition of the salaried middle class and peasantry, although it did not go far enough to fully satisfy peasant land hunger.[13] Several dimensions of the outcome of regime policies bear mentioning.

1) The broadening of access to education is one primary dimension of social structural change. Schooling at all levels dramatically expanded. Between 1964 and 1977, primary school students and teachers more than doubled, raising the proportion of the school-age population attending from 58 to 85 percent. Similar increases occurred at the intermediate and secondary level. Moreover, access to education became more equalized between the cities and rural provinces. University education also became a widening channel of advancement. Enrollment at Damascus University doubled in the five years after the 1963 coup; by 1968 half of its student body was rural in origin, 41 percent from the lower class, and only 6 percent of students had fathers with university education.[14] By the 1980s, new universities in Aleppo, Latakia, and Deir ez-Zor, and twenty-five postsecondary intermediate institutes had been cre-

ated. Enrollment in universities grew from 25,600 in 1964 to 109,000 in 1983, plus another 30,000 enrolled abroad. The percentage of rurals with postprimary certificates doubled from less than 10 percent of the total in 1960 to 20.3 percent in 1970. Given the continual expansion in rural access under the Ba'thists, it probably at least doubled again in the 1970s. In short, education has become a channel of upward mobility not previously open on a comparable scale.[15] Moreover, opportunities for state employment also grew apace: total state employment grew from 22,000 in the late 1950s to 250,000 in the 1970s and 473,285 in the 1980s when one in every five persons was so employed, not including the military. In 1984 there were about 153,000 government officials or employees, 92,000 teachers (not including temporaries), and 130,500 workers in the public industrial sector.[16]

2) The outcome of Ba'thist interventions in agriculture captures another aspect of state initiated social change, the dispersion of property. Land reform demolished latifundist capitalism, checked the forced proletarianization of the peasantry, which was threatening village life, and effected a major leveling in the agrarian structure. Table 1 indicates the impact of land reform on land distribution. The reform broadened and consolidated a small-holding peasantry, but it neither established equality in landholding nor went far enough to either abolish landlessness or create a really secure and prosperous "yeoman" peasantry. Rather a "mixed" landholding structure took shape. At the top, the great "feudal" absentee estates gave way to medium-sized, more dynamic, agrarian capitalist farms using mechanization and wage labor. Below this was a thin stratum of rich peasants and urban investors. Together, these top strata made up 4 percent of holders, but controlled one-third of the land. A step down, a prosperous, independent, middle peasantry making up one-third of holders controlled one-half the land surface. Below it was a small-holding peasantry, which constituted two-thirds of landowners but

TABLE 1. Pre- and Postreform Agrarian Structure

| | Prereform | | Postreform | |
	% Pop.	% Owned land surface	% Pop.	% Owned land surface
Large (100+)	1	50	0.50	17.7
Medium (10 to 100)	9	37	15.30	58.7
Small (0 to 10)	30	13	48.00	23.6
Landless	60	0	36.10	0.0

Source: *Peasant and Bureaucracy in Ba'thist Syria*, Raymond A. Hinnebusch, Westview Press, 1989, p. 110.

controlled only one-fifth of the land. About half of these peasants were relatively secure, but the other half were minifundists, lacking enough land to support themselves without supplementary off-farm labor. If these minifundists and the landless strata below them — tenants, share-croppers, and agricultural wage laborers — are combined, these *poor peasants* made up one-half of the peasantry in 1970. The middle and small-holding sector and landless strata are joined in the peasant union – cooperative structure, which controls, protects, and supports the small peasantry — with credit, inputs, stable markets, and reasonable prices. The cooperatives have made land reform viable and are by no means economic failures. But they have not become effective vehicles of village socialism — that is, of collective investment and cultivation; instead they actually foster individual peasant development. While government incapacities partly explain the failure of agrarian socialism, the simple fact is that small-holders have no desire to give up their independence to collective forms of agriculture, and the regime cannot afford to alienate its own base through forced collectivization.[17]

3) The greater access to opportunity and diffusion of property effected by Ba'thism has reshaped the overall social structure as captured in figures that contrast social structure before and after radical Ba'thist rule. These figures, indicated in Table 2, and other available data suggest a number of major changes. First, there was a big decline in the bourgeoisie, not only in its wealth and power, but even its numbers, through downward mobility or exit from Syria. Second, although the state-dependent classes, including both officials and public sector blue-collar workers, at first only slowly increased, according to the World Bank, these categories had, together, grown from 32.9 percent of the work force in 1960 to 37.8 percent by 1975.[18] Third, a large portion of the landless agri-

TABLE 2. Syrian Class Structure in 1960 and 1970

	1960	%	1970	%
Industrial & commercial bourgeoisie	19,750	2.2	10,890	0.7
Rural bourgeoisie	39,640	4.5	8,360	0.6
Working class	159,720	17.9	257,380	17.6
Agricultural proletariat	182,720	20.5	130,400	8.9
Traditional petty bourgeoisie	110,900	12.5	216,090	14.7
Salaried middle class	132,530	15.0	234,930	16.0
Small peasantry	243,460	27.4	608,540	41.5

Figures refer to economically active population.
Source: Elizabeth Longuenesse, *MERIP Reports,* V. 9 N. 4 1979, p. 4.

cultural proletariat was transformed through agrarian reform into a small-holding peasantry. Fourth, the "petite bourgeoisie" of small self-employed artisans and merchants expanded. Finally, behind these numbers is a still more complex social reality; individuals—and even more so families that still operate as solidary social units—tend to bridge these social categories. Thus, a public sector worker may "moonlight" as a petty private operator, a peasant may work seasonally in a public sector factory, and a peasant family may pool resources and effect a division of labor in which one brother works the family land, another seeks government office or public sector work, and a third is set up in a petty business.[19] An "informal" sector, linked at one end to the state and at the other end to the village, seems to have developed. This amounts to a very large, rather fluid and overlapping lower middle-lower class amalgam. Indeed, if one considers middle- and lower-level state employees, small-holding peasants, especially peasant families diversifying their off-farm resources, and blue-collar workers with a foot in petty commerce, services, or artisanship to fall in the petite bourgeoisie, there are strong reasons for thinking this the dominant social class in Syria, not only numerically but ideologically—that is, in its effect on popular culture and state policy under Ba'thism. This whole development reflects widening upward social mobility, especially by peasant youth, made possible by the opening of new state-controlled or fostered opportunities.

This class development had definite political consequences. Much of the petit bourgeois strata are either state dependent or beholden to the state for their advancement: the Ba'thist state was, at least in the 1960s, in many ways *their* regime. The demolishing of the old class structure and of the class control of the landed-mercantile bourgeoisie over the state together created the conditions for the rise of a more autonomous state and a leveled and fluid socio-economic terrain exceptionally amenable to control by this state.

Syria under Asad: Forging an Autonomous "Bonapartist" State "above" Classes

Under Asad the orientation of the state changed decisively, from an instrument of class revolution to a machinery of power in the service of the raison d'état—state consolidation internally, war mobilization externally. Parallel to this change, the state assumed a position "above" classes, balancing and playing them off. How was this new state forged?

Asad first set out to accumulate the political capital that would have to be invested in this project. He broadened the base of the regime beyond its plebian core, winning the acquiescence of the bourgeoisie and the *suq* through a muting of radicalism and secularism, limited economic liberalization, and an economic boomlet that revitalized the private bourgeoisie. The urban middle class was wooed through political relaxation and co-optation. The 1973 war rallied wide sectors of opinion to the regime and endowed it with a new nationalist legitimacy. Finally Syria's new role in the front line with Israel won it Arab aid and loans, fueling a prosperity of which the urban bourgeoisie and middle class took best advantage.

The political capital so won allowed Asad to take the initiative in transforming the Ba'thist regime from a fragile Leninist experiment into a hybrid regime that incorporated and subordinated the remnants of the former within an authoritarian "presidential monarchy." The presidency became the undisputed command post of the state, concentrating and personalizing authority, and raising Asad above the rest of the elite and power institutions of the state—council of ministers, party "politburo," and army high command. Asad successfully consolidated this new regime through a complex strategy that took maximum advantage of certain favorable conditions.

1) Asad's authority is partly personal—that of the general successful in war and international struggle. He enjoys a unique personal stature among elites, respected for his combination of conciliatory pragmatism, ruthlessness, and shrewd audacity in the international arena.

2) He also pursued a strategy of alliance-building and brokering. He allied with senior Sunni military officers and party politicos. Anxious to placate the urban Sunni center— Damascene society —and the middle class as a whole, he co-opted significant numbers of Damascenes into the top ranks of party and state and many nonparty middle-class technocrats into governments.

3) He constructed a network of personal Alawite clients dominating the strategic levers of the military-police apparatus, which made him personally unchallengable, and which, with its special stake in regime survival, presents an obdurate shield to coups or uprisings threatening to the regime. Asad brokers and balances these various factions. Thus, he puts "traditional" techniques of rule with long roots in the political culture in the service of state formation: the cult of personality of the military leader, the use of primordial political cement— *asabiyya* —to forge a reliable elite core, the standing above and playing off of the segments of a divided state and society.

4) He has also maintained and expanded the institutions built under the radicals, and much of his authority rests on his legal command of them. He combines in his hands the reins of the three major power institutions, leading the party as its general secretary, and in his capacity as

president enjoying full powers to appoint and dismiss governments and military commands. Thus, he also employed "modern" political technology — party ideology and organization, bureaucratic rationality and hierarchy. The result is the emergence of a very complex but strengthened state.

5) The receipt of large quantities of Arab aid — so much "rent" at the disposal of the regime for elite aggrandizement, patronage, and development — gave the state a second economic base. Besides its control of much of the means of production—land and factories—it also became an engine of distribution. The state enjoyed enormous concentrated resources compared to the fragmented private sector and remained the main engine of investment.

6) Finally, the emergence of this formidable state was possible only because of the revolution preceding it, which leveled rival sources of independent social power, incorporated and made dependent the middle class and peasantry and, in breaking down rigid class barriers and creating a fluid social structure, eroded class solidarities that might become vehicles for challenging state power.

The consolidation of this state again changed the face of politics in Syria. Ideology and class politics receded. The top elite — the president and his close associates — ceased to take sides in social conflicts and instead sought to stay above and balance the various social forces — the Alawite military, the party apparatchik, the state bureaucracy, the co-opted segments of the bourgeoisie, the organized workers, and the peasantry. Inside the elite, ideological conflict was superseded by personal sectarian-tinged rivalries, debates over economic management, and above all a preoccupation with foreign policy issues. State policy-making, increasingly autonomous of societal forces, was shaped by reasons of state, more than either class or sectarian interests. Below the elite, class solidarities gave way to individual and group competition. With the demolition of class barriers to upward mobility, the expansion of education, and the incorporation of much of the economy into the public sector, a much larger proportion of the population acquired eligibility for necessarily limited numbers of offices, positions, and patronage under state control. This shaped a form of social competition, which put a premium on personal connections. Regional and sectarian ties inevitably became the route of least resistance in establishing such connections. The channeling of "rent" through the state reinforced these tendencies, generating rivalry for access to it as the dominant political contest in place of class conflict over the means of production.

The clash of ideology and class coalitions was superseded by the search of small groups and individuals for patronage, privilege, and redress through clientalism and party-managed interest group channels. In such a climate, sectarian identities tended to supersede class identities, making the Alawi core in the regime more cohesive in defense of its privilege and those left out more conscious of their own — usually Sunni — identity. But other "interest groups" expressive of class, institutional, or occupational interests — the worker and peasant unions, professional associations, rival arms of the bureaucracy — were also part of the interest group "game."[20]

The political formation created under Asad might appropriately be called "Bonapartist." Here, as in postrevolutionary France, a radical Jacobin period of class conflict, which incorporated a mass base into the state and leveled the power and privilege of the old classes, paved the way for a powerful state above society. But also, in its excesses, it precipitated a conservative Thermidor, giving rise to a nationalist general who led the nation against foreign enemies and promised an end to internal conflict and a new postrevolutionary order. And, like Bonapartism, the Asad regime, though in a sense above classes, was nevertheless a product of a particular class structure — one leveled, fluidized, and absorbed into the structures of the bureaucratic state.

Late Bonapartism and the Incubation and Constraints on Emergence of a New Ruling Bourgeoisie: Toward a "Liberal Empire?"

Even as the Bonapartist state was being consolidated, there were signs that a new bourgeoisie was being generated in both its "heart" and "shadow." Pragmatic post-1973 economic policies, heavily reliant on oil "rent," sought to stimulate growth, appease the bourgeoisie and the middle class, yet preserve the ability of the regime to control the economy. Economic liberalization further opened Syria to Western imports, fueling a consumption boom and the proliferation of a comprador bourgeoisie. Arab aid and Western loans were channeled into a massive development program focused on crash industrialization. Since much of this revenue was channeled through government, the dominance of the state sector was at least nominally sustained and even expanded. Yet the state turned over implementation of big parts of its development program to foreign firms and local contractors, fueling augmented corruption, as opportunities for embezzlement widened and webs of shared interests in commissions and kickbacks developed between high officials, officers, politicians, and businessmen. Black market operations were fueled by the virtual incorporation of eastern Lebanon under the control of Syrian military officers. The political and military elite, using its power to enrich itself, was being *embourgeoised* while the private bourgeoisie was using wealth to buy political influence, bridging the former sharp antagonism between state and private sector.

Within the elite, both the Alawis (with their unique access to the state) and the Damascene component (with its unique access to the bourgeoisie) were best situated to profit. The enrichment of the Alawi elite turned an element previously one of the strongest forces for radical change in the regime into a group with privileges to defend and a major obstacle to the reform of abuses enveloping the state. As a privileged recruitment pool, large parts of the Alawi community, in fact, have gone from the most-downtrodden to the most well-situated social segment. Through the Damascene connection, a regime that began as a rebellion by peripheral outsiders against the urban establishment was becoming a partner with families of old and new business wealth in the capital. Although other sectors of society remained represented in the wider elite, and although party recruitment continued to channel plebian elements into positions of power, the elite was clearly losing much of its previous plebian social character. Simultaneously, the inflation that accompanied the oil influx, and, when Arab aid dropped off, the deficit financing that the state embarked on, were eroding the relatively fixed incomes of salaried employees, workers, and small peasants dependent on sale of the crop to the state for set prices; disaffection spread within the regime's own constituency. Thus, new inequalities were rapidly replacing those demolished in the 1960s. The regime elite itself acquired a stake in the protection and expansion of them. The Ba'thist elite was being differentiated from its political base, pushing it in an increasingly conservative direction in which control was replacing the earlier stress on mass mobilization.[21]

These developments created favorable conditions for a major new conflict—that between the regime and the Islamic fundamentalist opposition. The Islamic insurrections at the turn of the decade were, in part, led by the notables of the ancien régime never reconciled to the Ba'thists and by scions of merchant and religious families, particularly from the northern cities, peripheralized by the growth of the state-controlled economy and lacking patronage connections to protect their interests. But the growth of corruption fueled resentment among all those left out. Sympathy for the Islamic challenge spread broadly among urban Sunnis, including the salaried middle class the regime had long worked to co-opt. The Muslim Brotherhood developed sufficient support to mount a violent and large-scale challenge to the regime, which it repressed only with great difficulty and at major cost. Professionals and merchants led off with strikes, *Ikhwan* cadres attacked government positions, and the masses of the traditional urban quarters provided the foot soldiers of rebellion. But the Damascene bourgeoisie and *suq,* enjoying privileged connections to the state and under its ubiquitous surveillance, did not join the rebellion. The massive state bureaucracy, incorporating major elements of the Sunni middle class, remained largely compliant and quiescent. The village remained pro-Ba'thist or uncommitted, and rural —chiefly Alawite—military units smashed the revolt.

While at the most obvious level, this was a sectarian conflict pitting Alawis against Sunnis, it was really far more complicated. Although the rebellion did, as the opposition hoped, widen sectarian fissures inside the regime, the elite—Alawi, Sunni, or otherwise—ultimately closed ranks to repress the threat from below. Moreover, with few exceptions, the constituency incorporated into the state — the army, salaried bureaucracy, peasantry, Damascene bourgeoisie, much of it Sunni—did not unravel. The Ba'thist state proved a more formidable structure than many had anticipated. It was clearly built of sturdier cement than mere Alawi dominance and incorporated a multitude of interests beyond the ambitions of a handful of Alawi generals. Moreover, the insurgency forced the regime to fall back on its largely rural or ex-rural mass constituency, checking trends toward amalgamation between the political elite and the urban bourgeoisie. There was thus a certain return to the urban-rural cleavage of the 1960s. The conflict between Ba'thism and political Islam continued in many respects to be an ideological expression of that cleavage. At another level, the conflict pitted a dominant state and its dependents against those segments of traditional private enterprise resistant to state control. Neither state nor opposition can eliminate the other: the former has proven too massive and commands too many resources and instruments to be toppled; the latter is too diffuse and too deeply rooted in societal interests and sentiment to be eradicated. This confrontation can be seen as a hybrid of class and group conflict, a mix of revenge by old class enemies of the Ba'thist state with a new group conflict, taking a partially sectarian form, over unequal access to the state, font of patronage, rent, and economic power.[22]

Despite the advanced *embourgeoisement* of the Ba'thist elite, a new ruling class has yet to crystalize, the state has not been turned into a mere substitute for the private bourgeoisie in the exploitation of the masses, and state policy has yet to be put in the service of capitalist restoration. Faced with disaffection on both right and left, the regime seeks to maximize its autonomy of all classes, playing off various social forces and avoiding any decisive choice between the masses and the bourgeoisie.

Abiding sectarian animosities between Alawi elites and the Sunni business community are a significant obstacle to the amalgamation—through marriages and business alliances—of their power and wealth in a new ruling class. The state shows no signs of the Egyptian-style limited political liberalization that would open it to a restoration of bourgeois influence over public policy, without which the private sector cannot acquire the confidence needed to lead a productive capitalist road to development. Rather, the regime continues to sharply control political participation and access on its own terms for nearly all social forces. Party-state structures incorporate a powerful array of interests with a stake in a "statist" course and still hostile or ambivalent toward private enterprise. Far from having recaptured the elite or having achieved privileged access to policy-making councils, the private bourgeoisie seems to have little overt, and not even much covert, influence on high policy. Statist and bureaucratic interests dominate over private sector ones, and the workers and peasantry enjoy some countervailing power exercised in defense of populist advances. Policy is shaped above all by reason of state—the power requisites of the regime, its need for control of resources, and the empire-building drives of bureaucratic agencies, imperatives that continue to work to the disadvantage of the still politically distrusted old landed establishment and *suq*. Indeed, the imperatives of national security state take precedence over all else, and the confrontation with Israel continues to block any radical departure from etatism: the military absorbs a large portion of public revenues that might otherwise stimulate capitalist development, and the conflict diverts private investment from productive fields into short-term speculative ventures and makes Syria ineligible for foreign private investment on a serious scale.

Finally, regime policy has yet to be turned against the masses. The public sector has not been systematically or rigorously used to extract a surplus from workers or peasants, and populist policies remain an obstacle to both state capital accumulation and private investment. Generally, public policy reflects a balance of influence between the interests of the old and new bourgeoisies and those of the middle and lower strata.

A state that lacks a firm class base is, however, by definition "unstable" in the long run, and must, sooner or later, be captured by dominant social forces. In the Syrian case, two tendencies, sometimes reinforcing, sometimes in contradiction, are subtly transforming the state—namely, the patrimonialization of the regime and the generation of capitalist social forces. First, the Bonapartist state, with its personalization of power and lack of elite accountability, is extremely vulnerable to elite corruption and power abuse, which by the late 1980s was assuming unprecedented levels. The state was being colonized, its branches turned into fiefdoms of the very force that guards its autonomy, the Alawi military. This tendency was counterbalanced only by the declining strength of its institutions and the apparently weakening control of the president himself. As patrimonialization deepens, the coherence, rationality, and popular base of the state are all increasingly at risk. Second, the conditions of capitalist restoration and conservative capture of the regime are developing. The Ba'thist socialist ideological impulse dissipated without creating viable institutions that could substitute for capitalism, while patrimonial tendencies, enervating rationalization and state capital accumulation, undermined etatism. On the other hand, private capital accumulation advances: the bourgeois family has been to a great extent internationalized, its wings abroad accumulating capital, which under favorable conditions could be invested at home, while in the countryside peasant prosperity generates a certain kulakization and the "informal" petit bourgeois sector develops parallel to this in the cities.

As "rent" at the disposal of the regime dried up in the mid-1980s and the state as an engine of development declined, while the private sector remained engrossed in speculative nonproductive enterprises and kept from power, a crisis of development loomed. Resource constraints and severe austerity forced the regime into a more extractive policy at the expense of populist ideology, peasants, and workers. The *embourgeoisement* of the power elite and the growing limits of statist development must inevitably start to reshape elite ideology and policy in a way more friendly to capitalist development; already joint ventures with private and foreign capital may herald a creeping privatization. The obstacles to capitalist take off remain, and the arbitrary and irrational abuse of power fostered under patrimonialization only exacerbate them. But the development of new poles of capitalism, some in the regime's own constituency, might ultimately bring a political opening to the bourgeoisie and the capitalist road. In that case, the outcome could resemble the "liberal empire" — the opening of the Bonapartist state to power sharing with the bourgeoisie-in-parliament, similar to developments in post-Nasser Egypt. If so, the historical function of Ba'thism would, as Marxist writers argue, be the promotion of the "transition from feudalism to capitalism." But it would be a more broad-based capitalism than that aborted in 1963.

Conclusions: Class and Sect as Master Keys to Syrian Politics

Class provides the crucial key that drives change and links the major stages in the development of the contemporary Syrian state. The rise of the Ba'thists cannot be understood except as a function of broad class conflict rooted in major social dislocations. March 1963 marked not just the temporary overthrow of certain politicians but the utter ruin of the old regime and the rise of new classes, a political registration of long gestating shifts in the balance of class power. Under the radical Ba'thists, the state, in the hands of elites shaped by the class struggles of the 1950s, was transformed into a plebeian stronghold of a class war against the patrician establishment and the *suq*. This revolution from above cleared the social terrain for Asad's Bonapartist regime, a state of mixed class composition, balancing between and above the classes, and, as the font of resources and opportunity, the target of sectarian rivalries, clientalist politics, and rebellion by the excluded. This state achieved some autonomy of societal forces, its policy shaped by a distinctly state interest irreducible to class or sect, while in society itself class politics was superseded by group conflict. But the state itself seemed to be generating new poles of wealth and fostering a new stratification system in place of the old one it demolished. No new ruling class has yet crystalized or made the state its instrument, but this may be the next chapter in the story.

None of these developments dispute the importance of sectarian politics in the short run. The plasticity of "segmental" political culture continues to have important consequences: class coalitions are very vulnerable to fragmentation. When class conflict recedes, primordial solidarities tend to reassert themselves as crucial vehicles and the cement of political action. But class and raison d'état are each at least as important as sect in determining elite behavior and public policy. Moreover in explaining political *change,* sectarianism per se gives little real clue. Indeed, the importance of minority groups, notably the Alawis, has been their role as advance guard of an elite or as class coalitions rather than as sects per se. They played the role of class vanguard, then shield of state formation; they now appear as both spearheads of *embourgeoisement* and restratification, and as the target against which antiregime class coalitions have coalesced. It is this class/state linked role of sect, rather than sectarian rivalries per se, which is by far of greater consequence for Syria's political development.

THREE

The Alawis of Syria:
Religious Ideology and Organization

Fuad I. Khuri

At the outset, two general points must be made regarding the concept of ethnicity in Arab-Islamic culture and minority-majority rule. Ethnicity in Arab-Islamic culture takes the form of religious differentiation and national origin, or both combined. The first, religious differentiation, is an extension of Islamic dogma by which Muslims are clearly differentiated legally from non-Muslims in Islamic states. The second, national origin, is a matter of cultural and behavioral variation: Kurd, Persian, or Berber versus Arab. When Ibn Khaldun wrote about the Abbasids, he used the phrase "the Arab *asabiyya*," meaning Arab ethnicity. Non-Muslims, on the other hand, are considered to be either *ahl dhumma* (the people in trust, the protected weak) or *musta'minūn* (the made-secure). The *dhummis*, who include Christians, Jews, Zoroastrians, or Sabeans, are a collective category occupying a secondary role in society; *musta'min* is a temporary individualistic arrangement between a free Muslim and a non-Muslim. In this sense, the Islamic community (*umma*) is a form of brotherhood that transcends racial, national, or linguistic boundaries. Islam is *sharà* and *imam'* — that is, Islamic jurisdiction and religious leader.[1]

If Islam is to be *sharà* and imam, it follows that a country is Muslim if it follows Islamic law as decreed by a Muslim ruler; this is so, even if the majority are non-Muslims. The ethnic religious composition of Syria, as of 1956 the (the last census that counted sects and religious minorities), was as follows. Out of a population of about 8 million (today, around 12 million), 10.66 percent were Alawi, 3.10 percent Druze, 10.25 percent Christian with the Greek Orthodox counting around 4.51 percent, and 0.79 percent Jews. This means the Sunni Muslims constituted more that 75 percent of the total population of Syria.

The Islamic state is structured to contain Muslims and non-Muslims as well, irrespective of whether they constitute a majority or a minority. The question is who holds power: *inna al-hukmu illa lillah,* "command rests only with God" (Qur'an 6/57). Suffice it to say, therefore, that the state follows Islamic law and is ruled by a Muslim. When Asad came to power in Syria he changed the dictum from "the religion of the state is Islam" to "the religion of the president of the state is Islam," a change that is perfectly consistent with Islamic political thought. This being said, which of the ethnic groups, the majority or the minority, controls power in Syria, is not at issue. The issue is whether authority is in the hands of a Muslim or non-Muslim, and opinion here is quite divided. Are the Alawis Muslims or are they not? The Alawis of Syria sprang out of an Islamic tradition that does not conform to the Sunni understanding of Islam. The following discussion illustrates the point.

The Synthetic View of Religion

The Alawis believe that all heavenly religions (meaning of course the Semitic ones, for they exclude Hinduism, Confucianism, Buddhism, and others from their framework) have been revealed to humankind in cyclic stages, depending upon human readiness to appreciate and accept them.[2] They express this belief in the concept of *al-dawr,* evolutionary stages or cycles, which they restrict to six: the cycles of Adam, Noah, Abraham, Moses, Jesus, and Muhammad.

However, the Alawi concern with other religions must not be exaggerated. It is essentially restricted to the concept of the cyclic manifestation of divine revelation, its timing, and the participation in others' rituals. It is related that they observe many Christian rituals, including New Year's Day, Easter, St. Barbara's day, as well as the Persian New Year, Nawruzh.[3] The scale and meaning of this participation has been sometimes greatly exaggerated, especially by some orientalists who saw in it an extension of Christianity. For example, whereas R. Dussaud (1900) and H. Lammens (1899) trace the word *nusairi,* the name by which the Alawis are collectively known, to *nasara,* meaning Christians, the Alawi sources trace it to *nasra,* meaning military expedition or support.[4] In the Qur'an the Christians are referred to as *nasara,* meaning the followers of the Nazarene—that is, Jesus who lived in Nazareth (in Arabic *al-nasira*) as a child. This is much in keeping with Arab traditions whereby persons have a *nisba,* a name denoting the place from which a person comes or the tribe to which a person is related. Jesus in Arabic is also referred to as *al-nasiri,* meaning the person from Nasira; hence his followers are *nasara,* those from Nazareth.

Other Alawi practices, including visits to local Christian saints, the use of candles and incense in rituals, permitting wine drinking while forbidding drunkenness, are thought to be of Christian origin. Lammens treats the idea of "spiritual occupation" *(hulul)* among the Alawis as if it were the same as the concept of "the embodiment" of Christ (*al-tajassud*), which it is not. One must always remember that many of the early orientalists came to the Middle East to look for the origin of Christianity and made sure that they found what they were looking for.[5]

It must be stressed, however, that the Alawi recognition of other religions through a very complex process of synthesis does not correspond or reflect this people's views of themselves. The kind of Christianity or Judaism they talk about is different from the Christian beliefs of professing Christians or the Jewish beliefs of professing Jews. The Alawi synthesis is almost entirely dependent upon the esoteric interpretations of some Quranic texts. All religions are synthetic in the sense that they all are new combinations of old ingredients. The Alawi insistence on taking a synthesis of previous religious dogmas, which they summarize in the theory of "the cycles of revelation," is indeed an act of faith, a given. They insist that their holy book, *kitab al-majmu', the* "book of synthesis," must be taken as a matter of faith.[6] It counts about nineteen pages, and contains everything one needs to know about other religions.

The other side of the synthetic view of religion is concerned with the entire cosmic order. It is an attempt to seek corresponding analogies between the esoteric understanding of some quranic texts and natural, terrestrial or celestial, conditions. Al-Tawil, a well known Alawi writer, says:

> The message of the Prophet Muhammad is an act of mercy which encompasses the Muslims, the People of the Book, the entire humankind, all the creatures who have souls, as well as the entire universe.[7]

The Alawis seek corresponding analogies between "religion" and the universe through a free system of substitution between humankind, the moon, stars, and other cosmic creatures or features. Indeed, some Alawi sheikhs, who occupy top positions in the religious hierarchy, have deep knowledge of astrological techniques, which they call *al-jafr.*[8]

This is not the place, of course, to discuss some of these interesting issues in detail, but it must be stressed here that the Alawis consider such knowledge "high religious culture," which only the select few would or should know. It is private, noncommunicable knowledge that can be acquired only intuitively and must be kept as such. In brief, it is inferable but incommunicable knowledge.

The Alawis try to establish "the unity of the cosmos" through a system of free substitution or transformation, again based on the esoteric meanings of some Quranic texts. They divide Quranic verses into two types: those with explicit meanings (the *muhkamat*) and those with implicit meanings (*mutashabihat*). Al-Tawil says that "every verse whose meaning is not obviously 'real' or metaphorically clear carries an implicit meaning."[9] Not all verses that have implicit meanings have controversial interpretations: they are given a similar interpretation by all Islamic groups. For example, verse 20/5 states:

The Most Gracious [God] is firmly established on the throne.

Verse 48/10 reads:

Verily those who plight their fealty to thee do no
less than plight their fealty to God: The hand of God
is over their hands.

God does not sit on a throne: it is the "throne" of authority. God has no hands, it is the "hand" of power.

However, there are other controversial verses that the Sunnis consider to have explicit meanings and the Alawis implicit meanings. Most of these verses, if not all, center around the position of the holy house of Ali in religion. For example, verse 67/5 states:

And we have adorned the lowest heaven with Lamps,
and we have made such [Lamps] missiles to drive away
the evil ones.

Verse 67/3 states:

He who created the seven heavens one above the
other . . . .

These verses are subject to controversial interpretations. The Alawis do not interpret such referents as "lamps," "heavens," or "missiles" simply metaphorically, as the Sunni, do, but rather as implicit indicators of the house of Ali, by which the one is organically transformed to become the other. In his book on the Alawis, Sheikh Ali Ibrahim al-Alawi says that "there are no less than three hundred words or phrases that refer in reality to none other than Imam Ali."[10] These include, among others, the phrase "A Witness from Himself" as cited in verse 11/17, and "The Great News" in 78/2. Indeed, a good part of religious discourse among the Alawis centers around the implicit interpretations of such Quranic verses, so much so that they use the word *'ilm* (religious studies) basically to refer to the studies that specialize in the house of Ali, otherwise called "The People of the House."[11]

The Stratified View of Religion

It must be stressed that the synthetic and the stratified views of religion are closely interlinked; one derives from the other. The belief that religions have been revealed to humans in stages, depending upon their readiness to appreciate and accept the divine message, implies that some were readier to receive the divine message than others—hence, the stratified view of religion. The Alawis believe that the final manifestation of divinity took place through Imam Ali. The concept of "cycles," which is originally an Ismaili concept, implies that revelation takes place through divine manifestations that, in turn, appear to humans in a dual form: through the "messenger" (*rasul*) or "speaker" (*natiq*), and the "base" (*asas*) in whom divinity is manifested. For every messenger there is a base: Habil was the base of the messenger Adam, Sam of Noah, Ismail of Abraham, Harun of Moses, Sham'un al-Safa of Jesus, and Ali of the Messenger Muhammad. This means that Ali and his house following him are the last in whom "the will of God," or, as al-Tawil has put it, "the source of the will of God," has been manifested.[12]

In this very special position that Ali and his house occupy in religion and the very special role they play in Islam lies the uniqueness of Alawi dogma. Alawis believe that this special position has been allocated to Ali and the people of the house in accordance with verse 33/33: "And God only wishes to remove all abomination from you, ye the People of the House [members of the family] and to make you spiritually pure." Thus, the people of the house, including Fatima, the Prophet's daughter, and Sulaiman al-Farsi, constitute the sources of manifestation of God's will and in this sense "they are infallible in their words, deeds, or intentions."[13]

The literature on the Alawis is somewhat divided on this issue. Some, especially the non-Alawis who wrote on the Alawis, such as Druzah, Shakà, or Uthman, place the Alawis among the Ismaili branches. But Alawi writers, such as Salih (1961), al-Tawil (1966), al-Alawi (1972), or al-Sharif (1961) always seek Shi'a Twelvers (*ithna 'ashariyya*) affiliation.[14] Nahda journal, published in the late 1930s during the rise of the Alawi state in northern Syria, contained many articles written by Alawi scholars supporting the second view. Under the title, "The Awakening of the Alawis," Abdulrahman Khair says:

> They are Nusairies as called before, and Alawis as they were called during the French Mandate, but they are true Arabs, Muslims who believe in the infallibility of imams.[15]

As a matter of fact al-Tawil uses the terms "Alawi," "Shi'i," or "Nusairi" interchangeably. It is not easy to assign the Alawis any particular tradition, for they seem to depend upon Shi'a Twelver sources for legal interpretations, Ismaili sources for social organization, and upon both in some ideological beliefs.

What matters is the way in which these different elements combine in a harmoniously communicable religious ideology, irrespective of the varied origins of its constituent parts. The Alawis are unique among Islamic sects in entrusting Ali and the people of the house with a religious role almost equivalent to the role of the holy books. This is evidenced by their insistence that religious studies are, should, and must be confined to the people of the house, who set forth the style of Islamic conduct, rules, and obligations. They agree with Shi'a Twelvers that religion has been perfected through the delegation of the imamate to Ali and his descendants after him, but they disagree with them on the scale of perfection. Al-Tawil says: "At the time religion was declared 'perfect,' a fraction of it was deliberately concealed until the present day to keep it private." He adds: "The concealment of that fraction of religion itself constitutes a part of its perfection.[16]

In this connection, al-Tawil goes on to relate the following anecdote:

> When the Prophet was called upon to meet the face of his God, he gathered his family and supporters around him and said: "bring me a pen and some ink; I want to write for you a text after which you will never be lost." Those whose hearts were full of hatred towards Ali thought he was going to further endorse Ali's right to the caliphate and therefore intervened to prevent him from completing his will — the will that would have otherwise truly perfected religion.[17]

The Shi'a Twelvers in general and the Alawis in particular have it that religion can be perfected only by the completion of the "will" that God had ordained. This is so because the will itself is part and parcel of the entire divine message, Islam.

However, the Alawis believe that the will was concealed from the common Muslim masses, but not from the people of the house, Ali and his descendants, which means that religion can be perfected only by focusing on the studies of the people of the house. They draw a clear distinction between the prophet and the Imam: the first is a "speaker" who delivers the message as dictated by God through the Archangel Gabriel, but the second is a "base" who is a direct "source of divine will" as such without "inspiration or intermediation—his words, deeds, or intentions correspond exactly to God's will."[18] If so, it follows that the Imam is infallible and his understanding of the Qur'an is in total agreement with God's. According to the Alawis, this role of the imam is what is meant by verse 36/12:

Verily we shall give life to the dead, and we record
that which they send before, and that which they
leave behind, and of all things have we taken account
in a visible Imam.

The will that perfects religion was passed on to the people of the
house person by person, and every one of those who had it, passed it on
to his infallible progeny until the twelfth imam. Afterward, the main constitution of the will was entrusted to "the very select" among the believers in the Alawi way who, themselves, constitute "the very select"
among the Muslims.[19] In other words, the Alawis, among all Muslims, are
called upon to know, or are "entrusted" with the knowledge of what is
concealed of religion, which, itself, perfects religion. Just as Ali and his
house were "selected" to know the perfected message, so are the Alawis
"selected" to specialize in the studies of the people of the house—a role
that perfects religion.

It can be deduced from the preceding discussion that the sovereignty
of the Alawi community is based on two formulations. First, gradation of
religious knowledge begins with the manifest and the explicit, and ends
with the latent, the implicit, and the concealed, which perfects religion.
Second, they are the ones who are called upon to know "the perfected
message," in this sense religion or Islam, through the studies of the people of the house.

The issue is much more complex than it sounds. Belief in the concealment of (the perfected) religion is an act of faith, a religious given,
which must be continuously sought; it is a perpetual religious demand or
practice. The term "concealment" here may also mean sacrament, divine privacy, or secret, or even divine existence as exemplified in the people of the house, the imams. However, this presents a puzzle, for the line
of imams was terminated with Muhammad al-Mahdi, the twelfth imam,
which means that the sources of divine will disappeared. But the Alawis
have it that the disappearance of the imam could not possibly cut off the
faithful from seeking to know the concealed; otherwise religion would remain indefinitely imperfect, which would leave the world in perpetual
chaos. The knowledge of the concealed continues through the "door"
(*bab*), who instructs people of what is to be known, followed, or believed.

They believe that every imam had a "door" following the *hadith* related to the prophet, saying: "I am the city of religious knowledge and Ali
is its door," or still another *hadith* that stresses: "Whoever seeks religious knowledge, has to rely upon the door."[20] The continuity of seeking
the concealed part of religion is therefore ensured through the continuity
of the doors of knowledge in human society. It is believed that Muham-

mad bin Nusair was the "door" of the eleventh imam, Hassan al-Askari, and continued in this capacity during the reign of the hidden twelfth imam, Muhammad al-Mahdi, the Timeless. As a matter of fact, the Alawis were called Nusairies after Muhammad bin Nusair.

The "door" assures the faithful of the continuity of the search for religious knowledge; he does so not as a source of divine will, as the imam does, but as a learned person (*alim*) who comes next to the Prophet in the religious hierarchy. The "doors," who are often referred to in literature as "the heirs of prophets," perform the same role as imams without having a divine quality. Here, the position of the "door" becomes equivalent to the position of the top religious sheikhs, and in this capacity the role continues one generation after another. Sometimes they operate in the open, sometimes clandestinely, depending upon the political circumstances of the day. Following the death of Muhammad bin Nusair, many "doors" or *sayyid*s (the title *sayyid* is given to those who claim descent from Imam Ali) came to lead the Alawi community. The most famous of them include Sayyid Abdullah bin Muhammad al-Junbulani, who established a special order known among the Alawis as the *junbulaniya,* or Sayyid Husain bin Hamdan al-Khusaibi who wrote the famous book, *Al-Hidaya al-Kubra* (The great guidance). The Alawi sources say that al-Khusaibi was born in 260, the very day Imam al-Askari had passed away, and died in 346 in Aleppo. His shrine is frequently visited by the faithful today.

The Alawi community after al-Khusaibi was fragmented into various movements and orders, each faction following its own "door" or *sayyid*. In the meantime, the Ishaqiya order had arisen. It was destroyed around the fifth century by Hassan al-Makzun al-Sinjari. In this Muslim era, Sayyid Srur bin Qasim al-Tabarani also appeared in Latakia, leading the *junbulaniya* faction. His revered shrine is today located in the Sha'rani Mosque on the Latakia coast. To these historic figures, the Alawis add a long list of newly-established leaders including Ibrahim al-Adham, al-Hajj M'alla, Shaikh Yusuf Hayy, Shaikh Ghanim Yassin, Shaikh Mustapha Mirhij, Shaikh Ahmad al-Shaikh, and many others whose influence in religious interpretations was far-reaching.

In summary, four points must be stressed. First, the rise of "doors," *sayyid*s, or "men of knowledge" is a continuous process in Alawi society. The last to emerge were sheikh Ahmad al-Jazri in Balqizia in Syria and Shaikh Umran in Tripoli, Lebanon. Wherever the Alawis settle down, there arises an enshrined sheikh, following the dictum: "God manifests Himself in the weakest of his creatures."

Second, the rise of these *'ulema*s or sheikhs is a clear witness to the continuity of divine manifestation in human society. This is commonly referred to among the Alawis as "the manifest [divine] reality" (*al-zuhur*), the personification of divinity. *Al-zuhur* may come up after death through the performance of miraculous acts such as healing the sick, fullfilling the desired wishes of the faithful, or inflicting injuries upon those who meddle with holy shrines. It may also show up in "persons" who unite the Alawis and establish their supremacy, which is what Sulaiman al-Murshid did in the late 1930s and early 1940s. Many Alawis, known today as the Murshidiya, thought he was "divine manifestation" par excellence and dealt with him on that basis.

Third, through the continuity of divine manifestation alone is the knowledge of the "concealed," which perfects religion, ensured. Otherwise, religion remains imperfect, in which case chaos in the cosmos prevails.

Fourth, the Alawis strive to know the "concealed" part of religion, the sacramental, in order to perfect religion, not to be "secretive" about it, as many outsdiers understand. They believe that their search for divine reality is a private practice, which they alone are the last to be called upon to do — hence, the self-image of being the "select" Muslims. Many of these beliefs have left a significant bearing upon Alawi religious organization, as will be shown in the following section.

Religious Organization

Religious stratification does not include only the hierarchic, cyclic arrangement of the heavenly religions, as discussed earlier, but also divine knowledge itself. As one's knowledge of religion gets deeper, one's rank becomes higher — and the higher the rank, the more withdrawn from worldy affairs. A sheikh withdraws himself from society not merely to seek solitude, but to be an ideal example of religious tradition. At this stage, he represents the consensus of the community, above internal conflicts and factionalism, however defined.

The form of religious stratification, the gradation of religious knowledge, is evidenced by the division of believers into two main categories: those who have been formally exposed to religious dogma according to a standardized procedure, who are known among the Alawis as the "custodians" [of religion], and the others who have not been formally exposed to dogma, who are classified as the "ignorant." Among the Alawis, it is believed that whoever reaches adulthood, the late teens, is recruited into the "custodian" category through a comprehensive religious fellowship, from which women are excluded.

However, the duality of religious organization is not derived from the division of society into custodians and ignorant, but from the separation between the religious example and the mundane standard; the first operates within the field of religion, and the second within the field of power and coercion, and the control of resources and interests. The first is an instance of religious gradation, the second of sultanic stratification; the two do not meet or correspond, nor do they stand in contradiction to each other.

Religious example among the Alawis is represented by two categories of specialists: the "sheikhs of religion" and the "sheikhs of the forbidden and the permissible." The first deal with dogma and the second with law. The first specialize in sacramental knowledge, the part of religion that has been concealed from the Muslim masses, the part that perfects religion. They are entrusted with the responsibilities of fellowship and religious instruction according to the Alawi holy text, *The Book of Synthesis,* the major part of which deals with the esoteric interpretation of some Quranic texts. Dussaud relates that the Alawi sheikhs whom he had interviewed used to say that *The Book of Synthesis* is "the foundation stone in religion."[21]

The sheikhs of religion (*shuyukh al-din*) are not all lumped in one rank, nor are they formally classified on a pyramidallike, bureaucratic scale with lower offices subordinate to higher offices. Rather, they are informally graded according to their knowledge of religion and the religious influence they exert upon the masses of believers: the higher the knowledge and influence, the higher the rank. In this connection, the Alawis distinguish between the local imams or village sheikhs, and the white turbaned sheikhs, who are very few in number and occupy top religious positions.[22] Few sheikhs who live in Latakia districts today, such as sheikh Mahmud Salih, Habib Salih, Kamil Salih, Abdullatif Ibrahim, and others, are thought to belong to this top category. In the contemporary religious history of the Alawis, many sheikhs have reached top positions. The list includes Sheikh Abdul'al, locally known as Hajj Ma'alla, who is the most revered of al-Hajj family, Sheikh Yusuf May, who is the grand ancestor of al-Hamid family, distinguished in astrological studies. After his death he was succeeded by his son Muhammad al-Yusuf who, like his father, had deep knowledge of astrology. It also includes Sheikh Ghanim Yassin, Abdulhamid Afandi, Salim al-Ghanim, who was succeeded by his son Muhammad Yassin al-Yunis, as well as Sheikh Mustaph Mirhij, known as al-sayyid, who is the grand ancestor of al-Sayyid family of B'amra village in Safita, and Sheikh Hassan Ahmad, the apex of the Mihyuddin family in the village of Jurat al-Jawamiss.[23] These names are often cited by people whenever they converse about origin, group affiliation, and personal identity.

The top category of sheikhs of religion, much like their counterparts among the Druze, lead a very austere, monastic life; they are "closer to Hindu monks than to the Islamic ulama," as al-Alawi describes them. Their practice of austerity and monasticism is well demonstrated in the kind of poetry and prose they have written about themselves or is written about them by others.[24] Withdrawal from society has a very symbolic meaning. Much like the Druze top sheikhs, they withdraw and seek solitude in order to be examples of consensus and religious brotherhood, aloof from factional conflict. The prescribed roles, passed on from father to son, especially among the top sheikhs, become expediently significant: they ensure the community of the continuity of symbols that establish consensus in a factionally ridden society. The Alawis believe that "a sheikh is the son of another sheikh," which means that religious knowledge is contained in family strains. The element of hereditary roles in religious specialization can likewise be attributed to the emphasis on the principle of esoteric interpretation and the knowledge of the concealed part of religion. If religion is a personal experience rather than an open and standardized achievement, it should be acquired privately through father-son association and not publicly in open schools.

Unlike the top sheikhs of religion who stand for consensus and the unity of the religious community, and who live in solitude pondering upon the destiny of humankind, the local village sheikhs, the lower echelons, are directly involved in upholding religious ethics and fellowships. My interviewee put it this way: "they uphold prayer wherever and whenever they congregate." Some of them roam the Alawi land calling for obedience and adherence to religious dictates, thus establishing crosscutting links between the various segments of Alawi society through a series of dyadic religious fellowships. They are distinguished from other sheikhs by wearing an unturbaned white headdress, the turban being a symbol of personal sovereignty applicable only to top sheikhs. Some of the local sheikhs wear no headresses at all, which signify the lowest status on the religious scale. The sheikhs of religion, al-Tawil says, are "as numerous as commoners," which may be an exaggeration but it does indicate the relatively high ratio of sheikhs in Alawi society.[25]

The other category of sheikhs (*shaykh al-shar'*), who officiate on law, "the possessors of the forbidden and the permissible," are essentially recruited into public courts that come under the authority of the state. In more than one sense, they lie outside the structure of religion among the Alawis: the courts in which they serve, although following Shi'a Ja'fari law, were established by the state in the early 1920s following the Sunni pattern and did not emerge spontaneously from immediate community needs. Should these courts be closed down tomorrow, the course of religion among the Alawis would not be altered either negatively or positively.

Religious structure among the Alawis is paralleled by a mundane standard rooted in power and coercion, and the conflictual control of interests and resources. The Alawi community is politically divided into several competing factions, some of which are based on tribal or clan coalitions and some on religious denominations or subsects such as *al-Shamsiyun* (the Sun People), *al-Qamariyun* (the Moon People),[26] al-Kalaziyun (named after the founder of the subsect Muhammad al-Kalazi), or *al-Murshidun* (named after Sulaiman al-Murshid) who appeared in the 1930s. It must be stressed here that dyadic religious fellowships are contained within these subsectarian divisions, especially at the lower levels of religious organization.

Tribal or clan divisions among the Alawis are numerous, the most significant of which include the Khayatiya, Bani Ali, al-Mahaliba, al-Haddadin, al-Matawira, al-Darawisa, al-Mahariza, and al-Kalbiya. From each of these strains, there branch off a number of smaller segments spread in different parts of the Alawi land. The Khayatiya clans cluster in and around Tripoli and in the Akkar plains in Lebanon; Bani Ali in a series of villages around Sit Yallo, Harf al-Salif, Bait Yashut, and Jabal al-Wadi in Syria; the Haddadin in Tartus, Banyas, and Safita cities in northern Syria; the Darawisa in southeastern Turky, and so forth.

The Haddadin clans trace descent to the Master Muhammad al-Haddad, the son of Mahmud al-Sinjari, who was nephew to the Prince Hassan al-Makzun, a very renowned figure in Alawi religious history. It is related that the al-Matawira tribe, from which the Numailatiya clan had sprung (President Hafez al-Asad is an affiliate of the Numailatiya), came to the Latakia area along with Prince Hassan al-Makzun around 620. It is also worth mentioning that Salih al-Ali, who led the Alawi rebellion against the French colonial authorities in 1919 and 1921, traced same tribal origins. Incidentally, these genealogical data are very significant in structuring political alliances among the Alawis today, as Hanna Batatu has demonstrated.[27]

However, the division of Alawi society into two broad strains, one based on the command of religion and the other on power and coercion, does not mean that the two stand in isolation from each other. Indeed, there has been much grafting or oscillation between the one and the other, especially at the top leadership level. Whoever emerges as a strong, unmatchable leader defending Alawi rights, consolidating their power and unity, maintaining cohesion and solidarity, is given a religious meaning and becomes a historical symbol. This is indeed what some of their eminent leaders such as Prince Hassan al-Makzun (1240), Shaikh Hatim al-

Tubani (1375), and some contemporary figures such as Sheikh Ali Salih and Sulaiman al-Murshid, have done. President Hafiz al-Asad may be on his way to this elevated position. These celebrities were able to combine the meanings of both symbols, religion (purity) and power; they are at once imams and heroes. In other words, there emerges among the Alawis at times leaders of some consequence who exemplify the unity between the kingdom of God and the kingdom of Caesar—a process that continues to reinforce the image of the Alawis as an independent, sovereign sect.

FOUR

Land Reform and Class Structure in Rural Syria

Sulayman N. Khalaf

Socioeconomic and political changes occurring within the last four decades have transformed the life conditions of tribal/peasant communities of the Euphrates Valley in the ArRaqqa region of northern Syria. The general sequence of historical changes has been a shift from a semisedentary mode of social life characterized by a subsistence economy to an entrepreneurial capitalist agriculture that developed rapidly during the laissez-faire period of the late 1940s and 1950s. Finally, new socialist agrarian transformations were brought about under the leadership of the Ba'th Party. Since 1963 the Ba'th Party, relying on mobilizational politics, agrarian reform, and the peasant collectivization movement, has restructured society according to a new socialist design while still accommodating the operation of a sizeable commercial private sector.

This chapter examines these changes as they affected class structure in the rural communities of the Euphrates Valley. Specifically, it examines the impact of land reform on the dynamics of social classes. Before proceeding, however, my analysis here should be encapsulated within the broader context of national economic and political developments.

The Village as a Barometer

The analysis to follow is based on field research done in the Ar Raqqah region of north Syria, specifically on the al-Meshrif landowning family in their village of Hawi al-Hawa located ten kilometers west of the town of Ar Raqqah. The field work was begun in the early 1970s and supplemented by intermittent short visits until 1986.

With its own definite boundaries and local history, the village constitutes a changing society in miniature, witnessing the confrontation between seemingly incompatible systems and forces. The village community, placed in its wider context, remains an instructive focus for anthropological research.

I utilize here the time-honored anthropological micro case study in order to generate and examine generalizations about the dynamics of social classes, mobilization politics, and planned change as they are articulated at the village/region level. My focus on the al-Meshrif family and the development of their economic and class position within the context of their village and the local region delineates the broader development of Syrian rural communities in the Ar Raqqah region.

When the merchants of Aleppo and other urban centers brought their money and machines to the Jazira and the Euphrates Valley in the late 1940s, they triggered a transformation process in the centuries-old mode of economic life. They helped not only in the development of the region and its integration within the larger national economy, but were also instrumental in generating broad socioeconomic forces that began undermining traditional forms of social relationships characteristic of tribal or semisedentary communities in the steppe and the valley.

The rapid mechanization of cereal agriculture in the Jazira and the extensive cultivation of cotton along the Euphrates have generated in less than a decade not only capital but also new social dynamics. By the mid-1950s landowning tribal chiefs, through their associations with outside agricultural operators and city merchants, had emerged as a new social class, nicknamed the "cotton Sheikhs."

The members of this emerging social class were able to perform "mediating" economic and political functions between their localized communities and the larger national system. They also began exercising control of new economic and political resources, which they effectively utilized to perpetuate their dominant position in society.

However, the Ba'thist revolution of 1963 profoundly transformed the whole of rural Syrian society. The Ba'thists exhibited a capacity to implement radical land reform measures and to develop an extensive mobilizational, institutional infrastructure. The Ba'thists attempted to produce new forms of class structure and community-nation integration. Consequently the agrarian base of the traditional "cotton sheikhs" was destroyed, and the mediating roles that they had manipulated to their advantage during the 1950s were eliminated almost entirely. This was particularly true during the short neo-Ba'thist period, from 1966 to 1970.

Now we can look at the village of Hawi al-Hawa as a historical register and more closely examine the transformations outlined above.

Cotton Farming and the Rise of al-Meshrif

Since this paper has a particular focus, my discussion of the rise and development of cotton agriculture and its entrepreneurial class will be very brief and serve as a historico-sociological introduction through which the impact of land reform can be discussed adequately.

Before 1950 the al-Meshrif families (represented by Haj Khalaf and his four brothers) lived in Tall As Samin. During that time their father, Haj Ibrahim, was successful in sheep raising. When he died, in 1949, he left a sizeable fortune. However, this fortune was kept among the three sons, Haj Khalaf, Haj Assaf, and Haj Hamad, of his senior wife. Haj Ibrahim had been married to three wives, and his other two sons, Haj Ramadhan and Abd, as well as his five daughters, received nothing from the family's inherited wealth.

In 1950, after Haj Khalaf had bought all his agricultural land from an absentee landowner in Aleppo, the al-Meshrif moved from Tall As Samin and settled in Hawi al-Hawa.[1] The village was founded in 1950 when the al-Meshrif built their first houses there.

Beginning in 1950, the al-Meshrif began farming cotton as a commercial enterprise. In gradual and systematic ways they brought their relatives from various places to settle in the village and work the land as *fellahin*. During the 1950s the early settlers in the village were mostly kinsmen of the al-Meshrif from the Ad Daher clan (also referred to as Ad Duwahra). However, the gradual expansion of the al-Meshrif's agribusiness forced them to recruit more sharecropping *fellahin* from outside their kin groups.[2]

By the late 1950s the al-Meshrif had seventy-five to eighty sharecropping peasant families settled in their village to work the land. The village population expanded to reach about six hundred people in the early 1960s. By 1980 the population had almost doubled, to 1,057 people.

It should be noted here that the economic life of many village families was not totally confined to cotton farming in Hawi al-Hawa. In fact, the landowning entrepreneurial family of al-Meshrif itself had other economic activities located outside the village — sheep raising, dry-land farming of cereal winter crops, and rental property in town. A good number of families belonging to the al-Meshrif lineage also owned parcels of rain-fed land in the steppes, in the region of al Faid, some twenty kilometers west of the village. Similarly, some of the families of the Jhamat peasants owned plots of land in their village of Ruwayyan.

From the early 1950s, the owners of these parcels of land usually rented them to outside agricultural operators while they themselves remained living and working in Hawi al Hawa. Sometimes local entrepreneurs like Haj Khalaf al-Mishrif rented such plots of land from his poorer kinsmen for the cultivation of winter cereal crops, wheat and barley. Some of the peasant families were able to keep a few sheep and goats in the steppes, to supplement their livelihood, which now essentially had come to depend on cotton cultivation. However, the material gains earned from the rental of rain-fed land and the possession of a few sheep never constituted a steady and reliable income for these peasant families, since both were subject to severe rainfall fluctuations.

In 1970 – 1971, the government appropriated all the land located in Wadi al-Faid and numerous other areas in order to develop a 20,000 hectare local project called "The Pilot Project." This project was for the resettlement of villagers whose land was flooded by the al-Asad Lake created by the Euphrates dam, and for building fifteen large model community state farms. For many of the peasant families in Hawi al Hawa, this meant the loss of their land in the steppes. Many families from the larger Ad Duwahra clan as well as others like the Jhamat were affected. It was only in 1977–1978 that the government paid these landowners modest compensation for the land it had appropriated from them.

A brief extract from the life history of al-Mukhtar Mahmoud explains how cotton agriculture developed and the kind of production relations that obtained between the landed agricultural operator (*muzari'*) and the peasants. Mahmoud, Haj Khalaf's oldest son, emerged at a young age as the family's agricultural business manager, becoming as well the village *mukhtar,* mayor, in 1955. Mahmoud's account also shows how, since its establishment, the village has specialized in the production of cotton for the national market economy. Thus it has always been integrated within the broader socioeconomic and political structure of the regional/national society:

> In the very beginning, the early 1950s, cotton was cultivated on a small scale in comparison with wheat. Gradually we reclaimed more of our land, and cotton became the single most dominant crop. The *fellah*'s share of the total annual produce was 23 percent. He provided his labor only. If he provided fertilizer, then his share increased to 33 percent of the total produce. The cost of picking his cotton crop was his responsibility. The *muzari'* (owner) was responsible for providing everything else: the land itself, pumps, fuel, canals, water, plowing, supervision of building and maintaining canals, and so forth. Before 1963 we had about eighty *fellahin* working on our land.
>
> Usually the *fellahin* used to take loans from me. They would

borrow varying sums of money—10, 50, 100, or 200 Syrian liras. A *fellah* might need to buy a sack of wheat for bread. His wife could fall sick, or whatever. I used to record what each *fellah* borrowed from me. In my small notebook I kept a page in the name of each single *fellah*. Later I copied all loans and payments taken by each *fellah* into the larger books that I kept at home. The amounts borrowed varied from one *fellah* to another. One *fellah* might borrow up to 10 percent of the value of his expected share of the harvest. Another one might borrow up to 50 percent, another up to 70 percent, and some of them borrowed far beyond the total value of their share at the end of the harvest. In such cases their debts would simply be transferred to the following year.

During those years the government did not intervene in agriculture. Economic relationships between the *muzari'* and the *fellah* were based on individual personal needs. It was contractual in the sense of establishing a personal agreement, but there were no formal written contracts.

The *Khanji*s were brokers, merchants, and moneylenders all in one. They were mostly from Aleppo. They supplied the *muzari'* with capital, with the conditionally implicit agreement that the *muzari'* took his crop yields to the particular *khanji*. The *khanji*s did not charge their customers with outright interest on the loans they gave. Instead the particular *muzari'* agreed to take his crops to be sold in the *khan* of his *khanji*. In turn, the *khanji* charged a commission of five to ten Syrian piasters for the sale of one kilo of cotton. The *khanji* arranged for the cotton to be sold to other dealers or to cotton mills and factories. Throughout the 1950s and early 1960s government banks and other agencies did not intervene in agricultural activities.

Our *khanji* was Haj Omar Tatari, from Aleppo. Previously my grandfather, Haj Ibrahim, was a client and a friend of Ahmad Tatari. When our folks went to Aleppo in those days, they went straight to the *khanji*. They slept in his *khan,* and most of their shopping and needs were taken care of through the *khan*. At that time people did not go to hotels.[3] We had our business dealings with his son, Haj Omar Tatari, whose material conditions deteriorated severely in the early 1960s, when the state moved in and put its hands on agriculture and marketing of farming production. As a result of this the *khanjis* were destroyed.

Class and Modes of Domination

Some of the major consequences of cotton cultivation and class formation within the context of the laissez-faire economy of the 1950s can be
outlined as follows. First, the dynamics brought about by the cotton
economy led to new socioeconomic formations which were associated
with the emergence of a combined system of (*iqta'*) feudal and agrarian
capitalism.[4] Such capitalism involved the agglomeration of large areas of
land into the hands of a small class of landowners of sheikh origin who
employed their fellow tribesmen as sedentary sharecropping peasants.
This was especially true of cotton-cultivated land along the Euphrates
and the Baleikh rivers.

    In the case of the al-Meshrif, for example, we see that in the process
of gathering relatives as peasants to work their land, they were setting the
conditions for the reinforcement of the traditional lineage (kin group) cor-
porations localized in the village compound. On another level, however,
the expansion of the al-Meshrif's agricultural enterprise led them to recruit more *fellahin* from outside their immediate kin group. As stated earlier, a large group of the Jhamat lineage were brought to settle in the village. Later another group from Abu Saraia (non-Afadla tribal peasants)
was also settled there. A social formation was being articulated by the
emergence of new socioeconomic differentiations. This greatly affected
traditional social forms, which had been based predominately on kinship.
Kinship as a basic principle of social organization was transcended by la-
bor/occupational and residential criteria for the support of a developing
capitalist agribusiness.

    A second consequence of these developments was the rise of a sharp
inequality in wealth and landownership. For example, the al-Meshrif established themselves as a distinct local elite, and their newly acquired
wealth and social position began to separate them from the peasants who
were cultivating their land. Extensive market-oriented cotton cultivation
along the Euphrates brought a radical improvement of the economic position of the sheikh stratum of the Afadla and the Abu Shaban. Yet, in
contrast, improvement in the peasant conditions of material life were neg-
ligible indeed.[5]

    The final consequence of the integration of the region within a wider
market economy involved the emergence of a new outlook. Tribal sheikhs
came to be motivated more and more by the attainment of material self-
interest and self-aggrandizement. Their interaction and identification
with urban merchants helped to broaden the gap in attitudes and values
between them and their fellow tribesmen. Around the mid-1950s these

entrepreneurial sheikh families were given the label of ''cotton sheikhs.'' In a sociological sense the label designated the objectification of broader material, social, and cultural conditions within which the sheikhs were located and identified as agents of an emerging class.

The capitalist entrepreneurial economy in the region generated a particular type of class structure and relations of domination and dependence. Tribal chiefs were no longer dependent on tribute collection from lesser tribal groups. The transformation of tribal sheikhs into large feudal lords and the subsequent enmeshment of this feudal lordism with a larger structure of the capitalist economy freed them, in a sense, from their traditional patterns of economic and social interaction and responsibility to their tribesmen.

Prior to the agricultural revolution in the early 1950s, the semisedentary tribal communities, like the Afadla, mainly supported the house of the sheikh by a ''gift economy.'' Such gifts were locally recognized, or in Bourdieu's term, ''misrecognized,'' as a right (haqq) of chiefship (mashiyakhyya). A lamb in the spring or a sack of grain at harvest were taken to the sheikh's house to enable it to exercise symbolic labor — support the guest room (*madafa*) and other forms of generosity that social custom dictated. This traditional form of gift-economy entailed close patterns of sociability and economic interdependence between the sheikh family or lineage on the one hand, and the major kinsmen of the tribe (*ashira*) on the other. However, by the mid-1950s those same sheikhs had become agrarian capitalists. The sheikh or subsheikh, who in a sense previously depended (materially and socially) on the gifts owed to chiefship for the upkeep of his *madafa,* became economically independent, and his feet came to rest on different ground from that of his tribesmen. The average fellow tribesman became a peasant, a dependent one. To borrow Bourdieu's words, the systematic objectification of a new economic order, in a sense, freed the sheikh from the ''costly and elaborate gift economy, which was encumbered with personal consideration, incompatible with the development of the market.''[6]

In their new life of affluence and position of dominance, the sheikhs and subsectional heads of the Afadla adopted strategies and patterns of social behavior traditionally appropriate to influential leaders. In their attempt to produce ''conditions of domination,'' which were still in the making, the ''cotton sheikhs'' of the Afadla not only started driving Cadillacs like the neighboring sheikhs of the Bedouin Fedan but even began employing what are locally referred to as *abid* (literally, slaves) as house servants and coffee brewers. They built many large guest rooms (*madafat*) of cut stone, with arches and numerous windows. Among the Hawaidi sheikhs of the Afadla the new roles, patterns, and "strategies of accumulating capital of honor and prestige"[7] sometimes took an exaggerated form; in the village of al-Meshlab, the leading Hawaidi families built six *madafat* each with a huge fireplace displaying elaborate sets of coffeepots. Six guest houses in one village far exceeded what was required for accommodating guests or outsiders, traditionally, one or two had been sufficient.

Such local strategies for the appropriation of symbolic capital are geared toward legitimizing conditions of domination of this emerging sheikh/entrepreneurial class. We cannot, however, look at such socially oriented behavior as for purely utilitarian ends. Such forms have, in the Weberian sense, some rational value in the tribal system.

Stated in other words, the *madafa,* with all its physical and cultural elaboration, is a structure that is traditionally meaningful. Under its arches coffee beans were roasted and pounded, clients were earned, and symbolic capital (e.g., honor) accumulated. It is relevant that some militant peasant cadres and peasant Ba'thists demanded from the state in the late 1960s the closing or appropriation of the sheikhs' guest houses. The *madafa,* they argued, is a concrete representation of the old order, which the Ba'thist Party had set itself to destroy.

The sheikhs' behavior in the national election of 1961 illustrates further this radical change in the style of consolidating their domination. After the breakdown of the United Arab Republic in 1961, Syria reverted to its earlier status as an independent sovereign state with a laissez-faire type of politicoeconomic system. The new agrarian capitalist resources and opportunities enabled tribal cotton sheikhs, who were running for candidacy, to turn to their newly consolidated material base for appropriating political support. Rather than relying solely on tribal loyalties, significant numbers of election votes were bought.[8]

The new socioeconomic forces and the sheikhs' increasing identification and close interaction with the national bourgeois elite pulled them away from their fellow peasant/tribesmen. Thus emerged their need to rely on their new family resources to secure political dominance.

The process of guaranteeing the continuation of their position of dominance manifested itself objectively in practices such as the intensification of particular marriage patterns, the buying of property and houses in town, and the provision of the best education available for their youth. The future materialization of the results of such investment in education eventually proved to be a great asset and of tremendous significance. The members of this educated elite were able to maintain themselves even in the face of radical socialist transformation and harsh policies carried out by the socialist state during the late 1960s.

The Ba'thists and Land Reform

Modernist parties and ideologies are characterized by their own instabilities and by their own movements in relation to the transformations achieved and the degree of change in economic conditions and political consciousness. Therefore, at this point in our discussion we will turn not so much to the broader institutional functions of the party as such, but rather our focus to its dynamics and its instability and development as it was confronted by the imperative of societal transformation and as it related to certain classes within the wider society.

I will look at these issues as they relate to land reform and the changing dynamics of class structure in the Euphrates Valley. The political development of the Ba'thist Party in Syria has oscillated between "mobilization" and "reconciliatory" methods of government.[9] We can characterize the Ba'thist political dynamics until 1970 as mobilizing, in that they attempted to change radically the structural and ideological basis of society. However, from 1970 to the present, mobilization has been diluted, so that we can speak of the party's capacity to apply methods of reconciliation.[10] In order to understand the process dynamics, we must look at some events that occurred at the local level, the Ar Raqqa region. Then I will focus in on the al-Meshrif in their village.

Under the neo-Ba'thists (1966–1970) the regime adopted numerous austere mobilization methods. The ousting of the older leaders in 1966 and regime's increasing rural and leftist mold only increased the alienation of much of the urban population and small, yet significant, elements of the newly dispossessed powerless class of old landowners and tribal sheikhs. Since 1966 radical mobilization strategies allowed the successful rise of large numbers of teachers, students, workers, and military officers from poor rural areas or country towns to influential elite positions.[11]

It was in 1966 during the neo-Ba'thist shift toward more radical platforms and political mobilization that extreme socialist moves were made against traditional tribal sheikhs, subsectional heads, and major landowners. In that year, for the purpose of implementing more drastic measures of land reform in the Jazira and the Euphrates, an expropriation committee (*lajnat al-i'timad*) was formed.[12] In the Ar Raqqa region this committee often, as some argued, expropriated properties according to arbitrary criteria, destroying completely the ancient régime of mercantile landlordism. Former big landowners like the Hawaidis and the Albu Hbal of the Afadla were left with very small parcels of land, while others in neighboring areas, such as the Muheid families of the Beduin Fedan, were left with nothing.

Traditional sheikhs and wealthy divisional heads were rendered economically powerless by the destruction of their material base, and politically powerless by denying them any effective or meaningful participation in the political process. One member of the Haweidi sheikh family told me in 1974, "Why don't you just relieve yourself of this long and tedious inquiry? I will give it to you in a nutshell. We were in paradise and now we are in hell" (*kunna bil na'im wasurna bil jahim*). I heard Sheikh Faisal himself say while playing cards: *bihalayyam falhitna lib al waraq* ("nowadays playing cards has become our cultivation" — that is, meaningless occupation). This bitter statement is descriptively apt in indicating the sheikhs' realistic perception of their marginal role in society under the neo-Ba'thist rule. Another sheikh from the Haweidi equated their present inferior political position with the coming of what is called the "unionists," referring to the Peasant Union, Workers' Union, Women's Union, Student Union, and the like. "Everyone has become a unionist; even women want to join unions."

Events that struck at traditional local leaders further illustrate the mobilization politics of the neo-Ba'thists during the late 1960s and how it affected the landowning tribal sheikhs. The event in 1966, locally known as "Colonel Hatoum's putsch," provides a good illustration of our point here.

On September 8, 1966, Colonel Hatoum attempted a coup d'état within the Ba'thist ruling party itself. His movement was foiled by the dominant wing of the party under the leadership of General Salah Jadid. The political ramifications of this movement sent a ripple effect throughout the country. The regime's immediate and arbitrary reaction was manifested in extending its arm far into the periphery to assert immediate control. For example, in the Ar Raqqa region, orders were given to local government and party officials to arrest and interrogate tribal chiefs and others who were suspected of being a potential threat to the system. As a result party-controlled local authorities took the matter into their own hands.

I was told by informants mainly representing the social class of tribal sheikhs' sympathizers that the haphazard and collective arrests were mostly guided by the personal arbitrariness of local officials and their grudges against individuals in the local communities. The local authorities could not produce concrete evidence against local tribal chiefs beyond the fact that they simply were dissatisfied with the conditions they were forced to live under. The arbitrary and severe state reaction against the traditional chiefs only intensified their alienation and sense of powerlessness, which in turn exaggerated their antagonism to the system. The regime under the neo-Ba'thists perceived the course of revolution in terms of waging a class struggle in which they classified other Arab countries in terms of an either/or formula of "progressives" or "reactionaries." Some of the Beduin chiefs who were still in the country were rounded up and interrogated. They were asked questions such as, "Why do you go to Saudi Arabia and other Arab gulf states? How often? What are your connections with these reactionary regimes?" I was told with a touch of relish that one of the Beduin chiefs answered, "We are not bad. We are simply becoming poor. You have made paupers out of us. We go there to beg, and they give. Give us something and we will stop going there. We will stop begging from them."

Sheikh Faisal al-Haweidi of the Afadla and Haj Khalaf al-Meshrif of Hawi al-Hawa were among the first to be interrogated. All the arrested were intensively questioned about various aspects of their economic and political lives. Many of them, including Haj Khalaf al-Meshrif, were even jailed for a few days and then released. Since the late 1960s, most, if not all, of the chiefs of Beduin tribes in Syria (including the Muheid sheikh families) have left the country. Now most of them live in Saudi Arabia; a few live in Jordan.

The following story, involving Haj Khalaf and his son al-Mukhtar Mahmoud of Hawi al-Hawa further illustrates the confrontationist position of the regime regarding landed entrepreneurial families. The incident occured in the summer of 1969 during harvest season, when al-Mukhtar and his father accompanied by two kinsmen went in their own car to check on the four combines they had rented for harvesting their cereal crops in the steppes. On the road they overtook a jeep, which immediately started speeding after them. When al-Mukhtar stopped his car, thinking that the jeep needed some help, he was surprised to see that the men were outraged and accused him of trailing dust on them deliberately. They claimed that al-Mukhtar and his father knew that they were members of the Peasant Union in Ar Raqqa, and that showering them with dust by overtaking their jeep was a deliberate insult, an act of humiliating the union men. A stormy row ensued. Then both parties went their separate ways.

When the men in the jeep returned to Ar Raqqa they reported the incident to the president of the Peasant Union, explaining how Haj Khalaf and his son had tried to murder them on the road out in the wild. Then it was brought to the party (*hizb*) and the governor (*muhafiz*). In no time the story of the incident ended up traveling through a labyrinth of local government and party offices until it snowballed all the way to Damascus. There a few months later it was presented as a case in which the old reactionary feudalist was trying to harass and insult the new Ba'thist peasant. The interior minister, who was also the commander of martial law in the country, wasted no time in issuing a decree for the arrest and imprisonment of Haj Khalaf for one year, with no further questions or litigation. The order came to the bureau of political security in Ar Raqqa: "The arrest of Haj Khalaf and his dispatch to be jailed in Damascus, plus the confiscation of his movable and immovable property." Police came to the village at night and asked Haj Khalaf to accompany them to Ar Raqqa. Neither the police nor he himself knew what the story was as six months had elapsed since the car incident.

Quick and intensive contacts and mediations through the governor finally helped in allowing Haj Khalaf to be jailed in Ar Raqqa itself. The incident was given different interpretations, and the new militant party cadres saw it as a challenge and confrontation to their own stand. The al-Meshrif see the whole story as something trivial but deliberately fabricated and embellished with the intention of degrading a family and inflicting it with material and moral injury.

To make a long story short, further contacts and mediations were instrumental in reducing Haj Khalaf's prison sentence to one month only, after which he was released. The important point is that people in the Ar Raqqa district and beyond came to hear of this story and relish it as an example of the radical politicization of trivial incidents.

The Village

The broad transformations occurring under the leadership of the radical Ba'thists are mirrored in further details at the village level. Since the coming of the Ba'thists the village of Hawi al-Hawa has been going through fundamental changes and sociopolitical polarization. In 1966, after the state appropriated about three hundred hectares of al-Meshrif land to be later distributed among sixty-nine village peasants, a peasant cooperative was founded. Since then tension and competition has existed within the community at two interrelated levels. The original founders and owners of the village land, the Meshrif of the Ad Daher clan, were extremely dissatisfied with the division of land by the government. As indicated earlier, the Meshrif had owned and managed all the village land, and had employed outside families and groups as sharecroppers. The socialist measures imposed under the authority of the neo-Ba'thist regime led to the expropriation of about two-thirds of the Meshrif land and its redistribution among different groups of the village.

At the same time the members of the larger Ad Daher clan, of which the Meshrif were the most important family and lineage, were in competition with the other groups in the village over the control and running of the cooperative and the collective. However, by virtue of their superior numbers, and most importantly, their close organizational ties with the Ba'thist Party structure, outside groups were able to take control of the affairs of the cooperative, including its select executive council. They also gained a monopoly over the political organization of the village peasant collective.

Similarly there was political polarization involving the whole community, which was mirrored in the spatial location of the two main conflicting blocks within the village compound. The term *sharqiyyin*, "easterners," came to refer to the Jhamat and a few others who were basically organized around the Jamiya, the cooperatives located in the eastern part of the village. They arose as an opposing faction against the *gharbiyyin*, "westerners," of the Meshrif lineage occupying the western part of the village. The upheaval in the village is enduring and fundamental. For example, in the spring of 1972 during the election for the executive members of the peasant collective, some of the Meshrif and their kinsmen went armed to the election place in the eastern section of the village.

During the early 1970s factionalism was not confined to the economic and political spheres, but was having a fundamental effect on the village's social unity as well. Indeed, the very usage of the terms *sharqiyyin* and *gharbiyyin* indicates the sharp increase in social distance, cleavage, competition, and conflict. There is minimal social interaction between the two village camps, but most importantly, the village has lost its traditional personality as a unified moral community. It has come to be divided into two camps, each revolving around a different power base, each having its own anchorage and supporting symbols.

The Jhamat and other splinter peasant families, who were and still are in control of the Jam'iyya, have their links of support within the peasants' union and affiliations, but both factions are subordinate to the authority and influence of the Ba'thist local elite. Now, in both a practical and an ideological sense, the village has no recognized headman or leader. Leadership has become fragmented, paralleling the same process in the social structure of the village community itself.

All the statements mentioned above by sheikhs or events involving them indicate the extensive breadth of mobilization politics, and the severity of the dislocations and transformations that have occurred, as well as the dissatisfaction of the old landed sheikh class. They also indicate that instead of widening its social structure by incorporating traditional social groupings and interests in both the urban and rural areas, the neo-Ba'thists opted for an uncompromising approval that emphasized confrontational strategies vis-à-vis traditionally influential and landed segments in society. By being rendered politically impotent, traditional leaders and agricultural entrepreneurs were degraded and alienated from the mainstream of political and economic life.[13]

In addition to the severe impact of land reform, it is appropriate to mention here that the practice of the Islamic law of inheritance (which in theory at least divides property equally among children) acted to slowly fragment and decrease the size of land holdings in such landed large families. This gradual effect is already becoming noticeable among al-Meshrif families as large numbers of their young men are now building their own nuclear families. This effect is also reflected in the new phenomenon of these families having their own school, and university boys working on land during school holidays.

The peasants, on the other hand, succeeded in receiving noticeable gains. Their political position as the largest class in society has been given new strength, while the conditions of their material life have been ameliorated in relative terms. Salame points out that the existing Ba'thist system has established with the peasantry a successful political covenant, which to a large extent accounts for its stability. He writes:

> There exist a large number of peasant/farmers who at present are capable of identifying with the ruling elite which every one knows has peasant origins. The existing regime has in noticeable ways improved the conditions of these important and most oppressed large social categories. Moreover, the peasants remain the main source from which comes the staffing of the army, the party, and the populist organizations. In his relationship with the state the *fellah* has made big steps forward since the day in which Akram al-Hourani opened up in Damascus a small office for formulating and following up on peasant demands to this present day, when it has become hard to find one single urbanite in the heart of the ruling military political elite.[14]

On the economic front the new picture that emerged with the implementation of agrarian reforms in the late 1960s shows some improvements in the life conditions of the peasant. Hinnebusch describes this picture in statistical terms in which new changes have occured in landholdings and relations of production throughout rural Syria. A note shows the extent to which the reform of land tenure and distribution has been achieved:

> About 23% of the cultivated surface has been transferred to peasant beneficiaries and another 20% to State control. ... Big property has been reduced from 50% of the land surface to about 8% to 10% while the proportion held by small holders has in-

creased from 25% to about 50%. The proportion of the landless peasants has decreased from 65% to 70% to about one-third. There has also been reform of the conditions of tenure effected through an Agrarian Relations Law which gives the peasants an increased share of the product and virtual security of tenure.[15]

The Crisis

The neo-Ba'thists, as the single party-state, emerged during the late 1960s as the only institution having full control over the means and forms of violence in Syrian society. Their excessive reliance on mobilization strategies of social struggle seriously weakened its structure from within, and weakened the capacities of its leadership to achieve significant socio-economic development. It appears that the regime ultimately fell victim to its own political discourse, its own extremist methods that alienated traditional and tribal elements rather than recruiting them. The neo-Ba'thists became so dependent upon the active left simply to survive that they could not afford to impose the unpopular measures necessary for sound economic development. Yet without such development the very legitimacy of the regime was called into question. A serious legitimacy crisis occurred with the party itself, and extended far beyond into society as a whole. The crisis was resolved by the triumph of the more moderate wing within the party itself.

The Corrective Movement in the Ba'thist Party since 1970

The victory of this wing under Hafiz al-Asad in 1970 meant, in Apter's terms, less reliance on mobilization strategies and the acceptance of conciliatory methods and orientation within the Ba'thist broader political framework. It meant the suspension of social struggle and the abandonment of further mobilization politics and radical reform in order to forge what the al-Asad leadership called national or "domestic unity" to spur genuine development and strengthen national defense.

On the economic front the policies of the new leadership meant the effective abandonment of the drive to make the "socialist" sectors the clearly dominant forces in the countryside. In Syria at large, the economy became divided into two sectors: one of large capital units controlled by the state and another of smaller capitalist units under private control.[16]

Radical tendencies within the popular organizations (workers' union, peasants' union, etc.) were somewhat curtailed. For example, within the

General Union of Peasants there was a tendency for well-off peasants to assume leadership positions. These "middle peasants" enjoyed the opportunity to give each other preferential treatment in many interrelated areas, a situation fostering corruption, which in turn affected the union's capacity to be a force for radical change. The Asad regime, by refusing to intervene to correct this tendency, actually facilitated the deradicalization of the peasant unions.[17]

The various councils are primarily not to deal with politics but only with day-to-day economic, social, and cultural affairs and problems, thus appearing to have a built-in process of depoliticization of the voice of popular organizations in favor of more technical and pragmatic considerations.

In the areas of elite recruitment and policy formulation, the Asad regime also appears to have developed new capacities to go beyond the strict mobilizing criteria of social struggle set previously by the neo-Ba'thist leadership. Also, "the mass-enrollment campaigns persuaded a great many of the Raqqa townsmen and villagers to join the Ba'th party."[18] Young and well-educated members of the once landed sheikh class became able to join the ranks of the Ba'thist Party and gradually to occupy elite political positions at the regional level, and to a lesser extent at the national level as well. For example, Sheikh Faisal al-Haweidi's brother, Ustaz Abdul Razzaq, was first elected in March 1972 as a member in the Council of Local Administration of Ar Raqqa, and later in 1978 as a member of the *majlis al-sha'b,* people's council, Syria's Ba'th-dominated parliament. Ustaz Hussein al-Assaf al-Meshrif, with a degree in law, became, for a short while, a lawyer for the peasant union in the Muhafaza of Ar Raqqa, the same organization that only a few years before had attempted to obliterate his "old feudal family." In the late 1970s he occupied an important administrative position as director of a party/state-controlled *muassassa* organization for the sale and distribution of construction materials in the government of Ar Raqqa. Hussein was also elected a member of the local government council.

Since the mid-1970s the tension between the economically weakened and politically dispossessed traditional elite and the new elite groups has ceased somewhat, mainly as a result of the more liberal policies of the new regime of al-Asad with its attention to rebuilding what is being referred to as "domestic unity" within Syrian society at large. There are signs too that the old elite is beginning to accept the permanence of the new situation, which, from its standpoint, represents a marked improvement in comparision with the conditions it experienced in the late 1970s. Moreover, two and a half decades of Ba'thist socialist rule has also left "durable consequences" in the very fabric of contemporary Syrian rural society.

FIVE

The Emancipation of Women in Contemporary Syrian Literature

Salih J. Altoma

I have only recently understood why I feel more peaceful when I am cleaning, ironing, or cooking than I do when I am reading or writing, though incomparably I prefer the latter two activities: I once caught myself thinking how happy my husband is when he finds me working like a "normal woman" at home. Over 45 years after Virginia Woolf's death, we women are still the prisoners of the stereotyped "normality" moulded for us by men. . . . So often I come out of the university feeling proud of the way I have explained Shelley's "Ode to the West Wind" or Arthur Miller's *The Crucible,* yet on my way home the high, professional spirit starts to shrink within me until, by the time I open the door of my flat, I feel as though I'm a bad cook and, to some extent, a bit of a failure as a housewife.

—Bouthaina Shaaban

I began to believe that the sexual revolution (i.e., blasting our traditional concepts about chastity and morality) is an indivisible part of the Arab individual's revolution to wrest his other freedoms; political, economic, freedom of speech, writing, and thought. . . . That there is no salvation without a struggle against the various concepts including those regarding sex.

—Ghadah al-Samman

79

Three general studies concerned with feminism and the family in Syria provide us with an overview of the central issues facing women and the progress they have made in recent decades. They are: *Feminism in Syrian School Textbooks, (an-niswiyya fi'l-kitab as-suri al-madrasi)*, Damascus, 1978; *The Syrian Arab Woman in the Woman's International Decade (al-mar'a al arabiyya as-suriyya fi'agd al-mar'a ad-dawli 1975–1985)*, and *The Structure and Functions of the Arab Family (tarkib al-a'ila al-arabiyya wa waza'ifuha)*, Damascus, 1976.

The first attempts to evaluate feminism as reflected in Syrian textbooks used in primary (36 books) and secondary (32 books) schools between 1967 and 1976. Focusing on four broad subjects—women and politics, the family, women and work, and sex education — the book identifies a mosaic image of the Syrian woman as defined or promoted by various textbooks. There are passages that emphasize equality among married women in society, progress made toward woman's emancipation, women's heroic participation in national struggle, and greater participation in public life. Certain passages tend to reflect or revolve around pertinent views of the Ba'th Party's philosophy: "The complete pursuit of popular democracy will remain incomplete as long as women are secluded from society's public life." And there are articles of the Syrian Constitution, which declare, for example, in article 45 that "the State guarantees for the woman all opportunities which provide her with complete and active participation in economic, cultural, social, and political life, and it (the state) works for eliminating restrictions which prevent her development and participation in building socialist Arab Society."[1]

However, the study finds numerous inconsistencies that disseminate traditional or conservative notions favoring women's domestic functions and their complete submissiveness or obedience to the male members of their families as well as segregated employment. Issues or practices such as "arranged marriage," "dowry," "polygamy," father-brother domination in relation to wife, daughter, or sister, and separation between men and women are generally discussed in accordance with traditional norms. According to the author, rarely does the reader find an open and sustained critique of the traditional practices that perpetuate women's subservient status, whether at home or in public life.[2]

The second book, *The Syrian Arab Woman in the Woman's International Decade,* is an official government document interested in underscoring women's achievements in pursuit of their rights during the women's international decade, 1975–1985. Among the significant indications of progress is the law of compulsory primary education, which contributed toward decreasing illiteracy (among women) from 64 percent (1975) to 49 percent (1983); the relative rise in women's employment (in private and public sectors) from 9 percent to 16 percent (though this ratio is viewed as far below the desirable level); the participation of women in all professions/vocations except those regarded as "harmful" or physically demanding (e.g., the mining industry); and the greater role that women assumed in the Ba'th party organization, government, and parliament.[3] As George Tarabishi suggests in his preface to this book, women's progress is still impaired by deeply-rooted traditions and man's own traditional mentality. Referring to the latter in particular, Tarabishi remarks that no significant progress can be achieved toward women's emancipation unless men begin emancipating themselves and consider their rights as men. "It is not sufficient to declare woman's right to equality, but we (men) must also seek genuinely this equality, just as women should do."[4]

The third book, by al-Akhras, professor of sociology at the University of Damascus, presents the findings of his field work, investigating the family's structure and functions on the basis of four hundred families in Damascus. Covered in the survey are practices and trends relevant to marriage, polygamy, education, the veiling system (before and after marriage), birth control, and working women. Highly significant and detailed in its statistical revelations, the study demonstrates how wide the gap still is between the realities and the ideals of women's emancipation, notwithstanding the progress made toward the latter. Although positive changes have taken place with regard to women's education, their participation in public life and marriage practices, there are indications suggesting that traditional Arab-Islamic norms of conduct and attitudes remain prevalent. The study reveals, for instance, that only a small percentage of women (20%) go out unveiled and a much smaller percentage (9%) actually works. Such ratios or facts may have changed since the study was undertaken in the late 1960s or early 1970s, but in combination with other facts provided in the preceding studies, they point to the complexity of the issues that women continue to face, and the painfully slow pace of progress they have made toward emancipation.[5]

This is due primarily to what Nadia Hijab characterizes as "a somewhat schizophrenic approach" to women whether in Syria or elsewhere in the Arab world, an approach that "both encourages women to join the process of development as equal partners and holds them back in their place as secondary actors within the family context."[6]

As recently as 1985, Syria along with twelve other Arab countries subscribed to a strategy for Arab women to the year 2000 based on the Arab-Islamic heritage and the religious and spiritual values of the region. The strategy as outlined by a special United Nations Commission for Western Asia represents in essence reaffirmation of the same approach cited above, for it supports on the one hand "the right of women to choose their role in and out of the family," and on the other hand, gives priority to women's domestic responsibilities so as to "insure the continuation of the generations, the cultivation of values, and the transmission of knowledge and expertise from one generation to another.[7] Nevertheless, progress toward women's emancipation in Syria, modest as it may seem, is viewed, especially by women writers, in a positive light, undermining men's absolute authority, and contributing to the national awareness of women's concerns and aspirations.

Writing in 1987, Bouthaina Shaaban, a Syrian professor of English at the University of Damascus, offers a personal testimony of the newly rising consciousness that stresses "women's identity, rights, and ordeals." She declares:

> When I married my husband in 1981 against my parents' will, everyone regarded me as a social outcast. Even the dean of Al Adab College at Damascus University said to me, "Who forced you to marry an Iraqi and leave your family?" Now, in 1987, I hear only words of encouragement and praise for women who marry men of their choice, regardless of family pressures or social considerations.[8]

Haddad, in her study, "Traditional Affirmations Concerning the Role of Women," views changes in women's conditions in Syria as a development that undermines the absolute authority traditionally held by men over women: She writes:

> As more women seek employment . . . they are not only breaking the restriction of seclusion by coming in contact with other people, both male and female, but they also are flirting with independence. . . . It is reported that some women refuse to resign their jobs despite the insistence of their husbands. Thus independence breeds disobedience.[9]

Contemporary Syrian Literature and Woman's Emancipation

Woman's emancipation as a literary theme has behind it a long history in modern Arabic literature. From the mid-nineteenth century to the present, Arab writers, both male and female, repeatedly have addressed themselves to issues such as women's right to equality in all domains — education, family, work, and participation in public life — the evils of arranged or forced marriage and polygamy, and the hypocrisy and double standard of "Westernized" men in their relations with women.[10]

However, in recent decades the approach of the literary treatment of the subject has undergone (since the 1950s) a radical transformation. In contrast to earlier attempts, which generally tended to be conciliatory or apologetic in tone, contemporary writings are noted for their insistently uncompromising rejection of traditions or attitudes restricting women's development or their quest for full equality. This radicalized approach applies to Syria as well as other countries, such as Algeria, Egypt, Iraq, Lebanon, Morocco, and Tunisia, and to men and women writers. To illustrate this approach in women's writings, I have chosen three Syrian writers who have had their works published between 1959 and 1988: Kulit (Colette) Khuri, Ghadah al-Samman, and Bouthaina Shaaban. They seem to represent variations in women's perspective: the rebellious, the revolutionary, and the militant feminist.

Kulit Khuri

Perhaps one of the best examples of the rebellious variations can be found in several novels published by Kulit (Colette) Khuri: *ayyam ma'ah* (Days With Him, 1959), *layla wahida* (One Night, 1961), and *wa marra sayf* (And a Summer Went By, 1975).[11]

Days with Him offers, in more than four hundred pages, a microcosmic portrayal of the central issues that women have to face and resolve in a patriarchal society. Reem, the heroine of the novel, belongs to an educated and well-to-do Damascene family that displays a measure of modern orientation. Yet upon completing her high school education, she finds herself confronted with the possibility of becoming confined to her house like other traditional women. Convinced of her rights to equality and independence, Reem embarks on a course of action in which she challenges practically all established traditions restricting her freedom except in the area of premarital relations. She manages, step by step, to pursue her higher education, rejecting the notion that women in her country do not need it; to publish her poems in spite of the opposition voiced by her uncle who questions the propriety of her conduct; to decide whom she wishes to marry, inviting her uncle's disapproval, not because of any objection to the person she chose, but because she made the decision contrary to the customs of her country; to seek employment in a government department; to form friendships with men; and to exercise her rights in other matters concerning her life. In so doing, she demonstrates that an educated woman can and should take the initiative not only to question the rationality of the restrictions imposed on women but to free herself from the cycle of passive conformity to, and fear of violating, prescribed patterns of conduct. Realizing that society's gossip serves as a strong weapon against women in particular, Reem makes a special plea for abandoning the formula, "What will people think? What will they say about us?" in favor of understanding the legitimacy of women's needs, aspirations, and actions. In one of her encounters with her uncle, she asks:

> "The people's gossip! What would they think? What would they believe? How could my uncle be like the rest of the people? How could he take gossip and society's opinions as food for his soul? Does he not possess the inner strength which enables him to distinguish for himself between good and evil without being influenced by other people's opinion?"[12]

It is this ability to make a distinction between good and evil and what is right and wrong that seems to sustain Reem in her fight against traditions. Perhaps the most crucial test of her ability takes place during the long drawn out love relationship she has with Ziyad, a Western-oriented friend. At the beginning Ziyad, who received his education in the West (Sweden), appears to be unduly critical of Arab women for being "reserved" or "cautious" in their public life, arguing that they—not society —are to blame for their servitude, due to their lack of courage to emancipate themselves. As a model that he admires and advocates, he invokes the example of Western women as they freely pursue their personal life. Reem, though impressed by Western women's achievements, regards Ziyad's advocacy reckless and morally improper, for to indiscrimately emulate what Western women have achieved for themselves disregards the basic beliefs and ideals of her culture. With these ideals in mind, she declares, for instance, that "I will never assent to affection deteriorating to the level of eating and drinking!"[13] In other words a distinction must be made between affectionate friendship and emotional or physical intimacy.

As she continues her friendship with Ziyad, Reem manages to effect a tranformation in his outlook leading him away from the Western model to a norm more in line with her own society's value system. However, her triumph is concluded with an anticlimax when she refuses his request to marry her, preferring instead to devote herself to art. By so doing, Reem demonstrates not only her independence, but her conviction that a woman in her society is entitled to live as a single person, contrary to traditions that as a rule, exclude "singleness" for women. Her decision represents, in a sense, one more radical step toward total emancipation and equality. The novel *Days with Him* may seem to be excessively optimistic or idealistic in its portrayal of Reem's ability to rise and triumph against the customs she confronts. Nonetheless, it successfully delineates the complexity of the issues women have to deal with, including the misguided attempt to impose a model from without, the ambivalence of

Western-oriented individuals in relation to women's emancipation, and the failure of educated women themselves to stand collectively for their rights.

Khuri's second novel, *One Night,* is more modest in scope and less radical in tone than *Days with Him,* in spite of the heroine's extramarital love affair. It focuses primarily on the plight and frustration of Rasha, a young girl forced to marry at an early age (fifteen), enduring for ten years the anguish of not bearing a child, coupled with a sense of guilt for being physically at fault only to discover, following a medical examination in Paris, that the cause lies with her husband. Presented as a confessional letter that Rasha addressed to her husband, the story gives us, in a terse and highly poetic language, glimpses of her life from her initial resistance to marriage to the one-night love affair she had in Paris. We learn that her pleas for continuing her education were ignored by her father not out of malice but because of his concern for the future of his daughters. In Rasha's view, her father was "a good man, pious and eager to ensure a happy life for his daughters," but due to his blind conformity to traditions, and his fear of society's gossip, he was harsh and insensitive as far as his children's feeling were concerned. He says to her:

> I understand you perfectly well. . . . But what is the use of your studies? Sooner or later you will get married. Besides, people do not appreciate . . . society will fight you. Your persistent refusal [to marry] will make you a laughingstock tossed about by gossips. Your reputation will be besmirched and this in turn could obstruct the marriage of your three sisters![14]

Such traditional arguments in favor of women's sole or primary role as housewives seem to Rasha absurd and irrational; yet she is sensitively aware of their weight in her society, and of her obligation to bend to them, sacrificing in the process her interest for the sake of the family's happiness and honor. She concludes:

> I realized that I was responsible for the reputation of my three innocent sisters and the happiness of my family! For my father's happiness lies in our reverence for absurd traditions of which he was convinced. I realized also that, given my sensitivity, I could not agree to hurt my family, that I would sacrifice. So I said to my parents, "Choose the young man whom you like and I will take him as a husband."[15]

Rasha's conformist decision serves as a prelude to her ten years of unhappy and monotonous marriage. Confined to the traditional role of a housewife, Rasha sought but failed to find avenues of escape from daily mechanical activities. Her endurance of boredom was exacerbated by the fact that she remained childless and by her husband's failure to perceive her needs in other than materialistic terms.

As a novel of protest, *One Night* raises familiar issues frequently reflected in modern Arabic literature: arranged marriage with or without the woman's participation; the traditional notion that women do not need education beyond elementary or high school level, that the only role they should be prepared for and contented with is that of wife and mother; the insensitive treatment women receive from their husbands or other male members of their family, and women's fear of communicating their innermost feelings. In contrast to Reem, the rebellious and assertive heroine of *Days with Him,* Rasha exemplifies on the whole the pattern traditionally molded for women in a male-dominated society. However, Rasha's conduct, as portrayed by Khuri, betrays two basic flaws that set her apart from other traditional women: an excessively passive acceptance of her condition, and the unexpected adulterous act she freely chose to commit one night while in Paris. The latter, an obviously extreme violation of her culture's sacred code of honor, represents not only a self-destructive response, but also a negative expression, against stifling and outdated traditions. Aside from its melodramatic overtone, hardly justified by the intrinsic development of the plot, it needlessly serves to reinforce a biased but widely-held belief that women, if given the freedom they seek, are susceptible to moral transgressions. Indeed both the novelist and the heroine received harsh criticism for projecting in a positive way, or condoning, marital infidelity. A reviewer writing in 1961 suggested that Khuri and the Lebanese writer Layla Baalabakki were "considered in many quarters as daring and even indecent," and described Rasha as "a pathetic character through and through, but hers is a tragedy where there is no fall from grace, because a state of grace was never attained in the first place."[16]

Husam al-Khatib, a leading Arab critic, underscores the controversial nature of this novel and the outcries of protest it engendered because it was misconstrued as an open invitation to sanction infidelity under the pretext of personal happiness and existentialist pursuit of love and freedom.[17] Evelyne Accad, on the other hand, finds such negative reactions lacking in perception and sensitivity, as far as the Arab woman's reality is concerned. According to her, that Rasha is "a dead-end from the very beginning" is not her fault, nor is it an error on the part of the author, who has drawn a realistic portrait. Instead, Rasha's inevitable defeat is intertwined with society's failure to provide women with sufficient freedom of choice in determining the course of their lives.[18] Admittedly, a more careful and dispassionate reading of the novel will reveal, as al-Khatib demonstrated in his incisive analysis of the work, that Khuri intended to dramatize the plight of women in her society and the need for a radical change in familial and societal attitudes toward their rights.

The third novel by Kulit Khuri, *And a Summer Went By* (1975), brings out other dimensions of male-female relations, though the author has chosen, this time, a non-Syrian context. It revolves around triangular relations between a leading Egyptian economist, who goes to London for medical treatment, and three women: Jane, his English nurse, Suhayr, his Egyptian girlfriend, and Madiha, his faithful wife left behind in Cairo. Told by a Damascene female narrator, the story gives us vignettes of Jane's life pursuing what is regarded in the West as normal, routine experiences, but would be labeled disreputable in Syria. To have an affair every night until Jane finds her ideal husband is a natural phenomenon, as the narrator states, though she frequently discovers that the male friends betray her by concealing their relations with other women. The narrator, disturbed by such deceitful relations, digresses to reflect on certain facets of her country's values and customs, showing a familiar twofold attitude toward the West: a positive admiration of and search for the scientific progress it has achieved, and a negative rejection of what she regards as demeaning or destructive as far as human relations are concerned. Vaguely defined as it may seem, this attitude suggests that the Western model of women's emancipation or freedom cannot and should not be followed in toto.

Artistically, the novel is loosely focused or structured, having a number of subplots, and is marred by the obvious interference of the author, who digresses frequently to reflect on a wide range of issues, sometimes irrelevant to the development of the plot. Nevertheless, Khuri manages to provide a clear contrast between two models of women's conduct in an Arab society: the faithful, submissive housewife and the emancipated, single woman who seeks an independent life without marriage or a man's protective support. Representing the former, Madiha, the economist's wife, is endowed with the qualities of a typical traditional "Eastern" woman who enjoys her authority at home within her "little kingdom." She is idealized as a beautiful, superb housewife content with all her domestic roles, especially anxious to ensure for her husband a comfortable life, unaware of, and never suspecting, his infidelity.[19]

As if to project the wife's naivety and to unmask society's double standard in relation to marital betrayal, the novel portrays Yusuf as a man who has no qualms about his extramarital relations, or renting a small apartment for such purposes. Yet his love for his wife, we are told, never diminished one day.[20] There is nothing extraordinary about men's infidelity as a literary theme, a very familiar theme in modern Arabic fiction.

What makes it, perhaps, problematic or discordant in women's writings is the fact that neither the narrator nor Suhayr, the emanicpated woman, shows signs of misgiving or rancor. Suhayr, in particular, appears at ease in pursuing her unusual friendship with Yusuf, as a single woman following him to London, in spite of her knowledge that he has other affairs and the admiration he expresses for his wife. As a model for the emancipated single woman, Suhayr is drawn as a talented journalist, self-confident, unyielding, capable of independently pursuing her life, and determined to persist in her course without thinking of marriage.[21] However, she is keenly aware of her emotional needs, which she can fulfill or seeks to fulfill only through a love relationship with a man, provided such a relationship does not imply subordination or exploitation. Suhayr's personal conduct points, both implicitly and explicitly, to an alternative outside traditional marriage, an alternative radically incompatible with and alien to her cultural values. In other words, with Suhayr and other fictional characters, "singleness," which normally "disappears from the female population before age thirty" in a Muslim society, seems to emerge as a viable and legitimate option insofar as some Arab feminists are concerned.[22]

Ghadah al-Samman

Ghadah al-Samman (1942–) differs from other Syrian women writers in two fundamental respects. First, since 1964 she has lived nearly all of her career outside Syria, primarily in Lebanon, with the exception of several, apparently crucial, years between 1966 and 1969, spent in different European countries. According to her, these years were instrumental in turning her into a different individual in comparison to her pre-1966 period. Her European years provided her, as she says, with an eye-opening experience, traveling and working as a stranger in foreign countries, without the protection of "family-social status-money," learning what she never learned before. It was during these years that she experienced a series of personal setbacks: the 1966 death of her father, a leading Syrian intellectual, former minister of education and university president; a three-month jail sentence issued against her in abstentia because she left Syria without permission; her dismissal from her correspondent's job for a Lebanese journal; and her family's decision to sever their ties with her due to her determination to be free and completely independent. It was also during these years that she finally realized how banal were the values of Damascene bourgeois society, which regarded her as an irredeemable woman.[23] Second, al-Samman has differed from other women writers in terms of her extensive and multifaceted writings since 1962, beginning with her first collection of short stories, *Your Eyes Are My Fate* (*aynak qadari*). She has published numerous works (short stories, novels, essays, and interviews) that reflect her preoccupation not only with the oppression of women in Syria or in the Arab world in general, but also, more importantly, with broader Arab sociopolitical problems and the need for a radical transformation of Arab society in all respects. It is not therefore possible to deal with her only as a Syrian writer focusing on Syria's societal issues, or only as a feminist concerned solely with the emancipation of women. As Awwad's recent study has indicated, al-Samman's fiction alone, as published during the period 1961 – 1975, offers a wide range of sociopolitical themes concerned with Lebanon, Palestine, and other Arab countries.

Nevertheless, a review of selected writing she has published on women reveals a gradual shift in her perspective from an earlier rebellious, individualistic stand against men and society, to a revolutionary and activist orientation that envisages no solution for women's problems without a total transformation of Arab society.

Al-Samman's first collection is largely concerned with the ordeals of women in a male-dominated society. Among her themes are the unwelcome birth of girls and its distorting impact, the infidelity of men combined with their double standard of morality regarding adultery, whether committed by a fiancé, a husband, or a lover,[24] arranged or imposed marriage, and women's determination to pursue an education and professional career. Her story, "A Man in the Alley," deals with a theme revolving around the anguish of a young girl being forced, by her father and mother, to marry a man, she does not know.[25] However, al-Samman retells it in a new version, rich in its use of suggestive flashbacks and the girl's interior monologue. The anguish of the modern girl acquires intensity and depth by the allusion made to the tragic fate of her sisters, buried alive in the desert more than a thousand years ago:

> For the last time I look at my father's eyes angry, begging for help, struck by their glitter whenever a suitor knocks on our door. It appears to me that I saw him many generations before I was born here. I saw him more than a thousand years ago in the desert, digging up the sands to bury me! And I see him now as I am about to be buried in the chest of an unknown man.

Both the flashbacks and the interior monologues bring up other types of abuse: the demeaning character of the bridal dowry, the humiliation her mother endures submissively and her ordeal as an "incubator," and the neighbor's daily betrayal of his wife. Such negative projection of women's past and present condition is intended to serve as a prelude to the daughter's refusal to accept the same fate, when she decides: "I will never marry this man. . . . I want to complete my studies."[26]

With these and other similar themes she pursued in her pre-1966 works, al-Samman sought to expose, lament, and protest society's anachronistic restrictions imposed on women, and to focus on women-oriented solutions.[27] But in her later writings she began to realize that her themes and proposed solutions were too individualistic or partial in character. Writing in the early 1970s, she identified the shift in her thinking:

> I began to believe that the sexual revolution (i.e., blasting our traditional concepts about chastity and morality) is an indivisible part of the Arab individual's revolution to wrest the other freedoms: the political and economic freedoms, the freedom of speech, writing, and thought. . . . That there is no salvation without a struggle against the various concepts, including those regarding sex.[28]

As the preceding statement suggests, her writings in this phase are marked by a new revolutionary tone, unrestrained attack on most, if not all, traditional institutions, and impatience with the slow pace of change, or the partial, rather than comprehensive, solutions sought or proposed for social or political ills. One feels a sense of urgency in her approach, and a strong conviction that women's problems, for example, cannot be resolved without "a total human revolution on all levels: economic, intellectual, political, and social." It is futile for Arab women, oppressed as they are, to declare civil disobedience against men or to reject housework or childbearing, because, in her view "the Arab man himself is not so much an oppressor of women as he is a victim of the social and class structure in most of our countries."[29] As a result, the adversative relation between men and women, which characterizes her earlier themes (and other feminist writings), is deemphasized in favor of a conscious alliance of men and women in their struggle against their true enemies. Likewise, the emancipation of women becomes with her not a question of attaining equality with men, but a matter of greater significance: the emancipation of both the woman and the man in a society in which both are equally oppressed.[30]

Al-Samman's radical (and provocative) approach becomes more pronounced as she addresses herself to sensitive issues: premarital or extramarital relations, and marriage. To begin with, she seems to hold a strong view against her society's current moral values regarding sex or marriage. Asked once what she would accept of these values, she responded: "Nothing of course as long as the starting point is wrong, as long as each sex has the wrong attitude toward the other, and as long as this attitude is perpetuated by society's official and non-official institutions."[31] It is evidently clear that her negative view stems from her belief that male-female relationships are basically flawed by being exploitive, businesslike, and soporific. They lack in essence mutually shared love, devotion, respect, and responsibility toward each other. With this view in mind, al-Samman assails marriage as an institution that betrays or disregards "the essence of the human soul and its true feelings," declaring "marriage, in its present form, is a corrupt institution . . . often a kind of human fornication, endorsed by two witnesses and an official document."[32]

There is no doubt that al-Samman, by generalizing her irreverent attitudes, provokes, as she had in the past, equally irreverent and emotionally charged criticism, including the claim that she is advocating Western models. It is, however, relevant to add that, in expressing her antitraditional views, she rejects also Western morality as "a model" or "a highest ideal" to be followed. Yet she finds it imperative to have the Western model in mind, not for the sake of "implementing it in our society, but in order to help us understand our problem, and increase our ability to surpass it [the model] in accordance with our history and our reality."[33]

As for her views regarding marriage or the family, there is evidence that she, while admittedly tolerant of other alternatives, longs to preserve the family's entity and protect the human relations within it from frivolity and decadence, if only two key principles are observed by the parties involved: "responsibility and dignity."[34]

From these and other statements, it can be concluded that al-Samman's perspective has a universal dimension echoing women's concerns in the West and elsewhere. Hers, to borrow Rossanda's remarks in a different context, "does not limit itself to asking for access to increased rights and powers, but fundamentally calls into question their proclaimed universality."[35] She is the type of woman who seeks "to make of the historical experience of women a principle with which to attack the whole culture of the dominant class and sex."[36]

The highly idealized model she relentlessly seeks for female-male relationships is not only at variance with the current conditions in the West; it is painfully far beyond, and out of step with, the unfulfilled but modest aspirations of women in her own society.

Bouthaina Shaaban

In contrast to al-Samman, Bouthaina Shaaban (1951–), a professor of English at the University of Damascus, gives us a more informative, realistic, and modest account of women's emancipation in Syria during the last few decades. She offers it not as a novelist, but as a writer with a noted sensibility who draws on autobiographical material relevant to her own life and the lives of other women she has interviewed. Her recently published book includes chapters on Arab women in other countries (Lebanon, Palestine, and Algeria). But here I will focus on her autobiographical sketch covering about twenty years of life and experience, 1968–1987.[37]

Shaaban's story begins in her junior year, 1968, while attending a coed high school in her village. This year is recalled vividly because of a classmate's murder of his pregnant sister.[38] He murdered his unmarried sister in defense of his family's honor. It is not only the act that is recalled, but the circumstances that victimized the girl, who had been sent to Lebanon in support of her family, and the halo of heroism and respect her classmate enjoyed after serving a six-month prison term. Following her high school graduation, Shaaban was encouraged to leave for Damascus in pursuit of her college education. To her it was an eventful experience, for she was the first girl to leave the village on her own (unaccompanied by male relatives) without reservation on the part of her family or the village community. "On the contrary," she recalls, "the village people were talking with admiration and pride about my performance and my will to pursue my studies."[39] While at the university, she experienced two events symbolizing her limited freedom as a woman in search of personal aspirations: her love affair with a man she wanted to marry but who was opposed by her father, and the physical pain and humiliation to which she was subjected by her brother because of a poem she wrote.[40] Both the poem, which deals, we are told, with the double standard of morality, and her love relationship, represent, in a sense, an initial step toward questioning and rejecting antiquated values or customs, but without risking a rupture in her family ties.

However, as Shaaban proceeded in her Ph.D. studies at Warwick University in England, a significant development in itself, she found herself compelled to assert her personal rights rather than acquiesce in traditional family obligations. This crucial conflict arose because of her determination to marry an Iraqi student she had met at the university (like herself, pursuing a Ph.D. degree), and her family's uncompromising opposition. According to her, her father and other members of the family justified their opposition by emphasizing the "religious" and "national" differences that separated her from the man she wished to marry.

But in reality these differences were, in her opinion, only a pretext for a more serious matter—namely, the fact that she was the first woman they had known to choose her husband quite independently of her father's and brothers' wishes. Once again, Shaaban evokes the double standard applied to men and women by referring to the fact that her brothers married women of their choice while she, a woman, was denied the same right. Faced by her father's ultimatum either to leave the man of her choice or leave home and never see her parents again, Shaaban was forced to make the choice in favor of her personal rights.

Shaaban's personal triumph may not seem significant, given the long history of women's struggle for their rights and the progress they have achieved thus far in Syria under a secularized political system. But her experience is highly significant in that it indicates her society's limited margin of tolerance for women who deviate, modestly or radically, from established norms. In Shaaban's case, her marriage, though not in complete accord with traditions, can hardly be characterized as a radical departure. Yet she was regarded as "a social outcast" even among her university community. Writing in 1987 (seven years after her marriage), Shaaban displays mixed feelings of optimism and frustration. She admits that noticeable positive changes in attitudes or women's conditions have taken place in recent years. However, she still is disturbed by the legal and illegal restrictions that women have to fight, including laws that deny them the right to travel abroad alone, or to work against the wishes of their husbands, or laws that penalize them for acts deemed dishonorable to the family.[41]

Aside from legally sanctified restrictions, Shaaban identifies other grievous conditions to which women are subjected: men's capricious and authoritarian treatment of women, domestic injustices, the deeply ingrained resentment toward having girls as children, and the state of fear they suffer, often on a daily basis.

Being herself a mother of two daughters, Shaaban reveals in detail how biased both women and men are in their attitudes toward girls. "Topical stories at the hospital were of poor mothers who had three or four girls and were desperate for a boy." "If you don't manage a boy, all this fuss about having a family is useless. All that girls bring you is concern and worry; there is nothing like having a boy and feeling confident that he can go to the end of the earth and come back safely."[42] However, it is "fear" that seems to be the focal point in women's suffering, "the thing that distorts most women's characters," ranging from an extreme case of fearing physical punishment to a more ordinary and daily fear of failure to perform adequately their domestic duties. Alluding to her own experience, Shaaban writes: "I was often living in a state of fear lest I was discovered bleeding, writing a poem, choosing a husband. I even lived in fear of becoming pregnant with a girl rather than a boy." It is interesting to note that widows, on the whole, are relieved of the fears she describes; they appear to her to be more cheerful, more confident, strong, and in control of their lives, whereas married women appear subdued, less confident under emotional stress, and sometimes reduced to feeble creatures by the mere presence of their husbands.[43]

In comparing Shaaban's approach to women's issues with that of al-Samman, several striking differences can be noted. First, Shaaban is more concerned with women's essential rights in the areas of education, work, freedom to pursue their personal aspirations, and equal and respectful treatment at home and in society. She avoids sensitive or controversial issues such as premarital or sexual relations, and other forms of behavior that are diametrically opposed to her society's basic values. Her attitude, as mentioned earlier, is more cautious or restrained, being aware of the constraints within which it can operate constructively, at the current phase of women's emancipation. Second, in marked contrast to al-Samman's admonition against targeting only men as the enemy, Shaaban seems to be following precisely the path her compatriot had rejected. She is excessively overtaken by her rage against men, "almost all men," to use her words; fathers, husbands, brothers, and others. They are condemned for their many sins: their tyranny, hypocrisy, double standards, exploitation, or fear of true female strength. Nowhere does she seem to be interested in exploring the socioeconomic and political roots of their behavior or of oppression, whether in relation to male or female members of her society. Nor does she project any redeeming qualities in the men's world aside from vague references to the noticeable changes in attitudes she has observed in recent years. The last few words in her account sum up her feelings:

> I am angry with male hypocrites — and that includes almost all men — who try to propagate the idea that, just because women go out to work, to school or to university, they are now fully liberated and independent. The aim of these hypocrites is to make women feel grateful for the slight progress they have made and stop them from going beyond this. Yet the real battle has only just begun.[44]

Finally, she conceives of her battle as one against men and not in alliance with them against their common enemy, as al-Samman suggests. In her concluding observation, in answer to her question "And now what?" she urges women not to fight men's battles while losing out themselves, to be aware of the more subtle battles beyond the legal ones that women should continue to fight, to seek the political power they failed to gain in the past. They should seek "to spread a feminist consciousness in every domain and across all social categories.'' Her solutions may lead to greater power for women, but in the process may subvert the possibility of evolving a total bisexual culture free of deeply rooted tension and inequality between men and women.

This brief survey, selective as it is, leads me to underline a few points made in the course of my discussion of women's emancipation in Syria. First, it is evident that, in spite of the progress made toward equality, especially in educational and work opportunities, Syrian women are still confronted with biases or customs that limit their ability to pursue their legitimate aspirations. Perhaps it would be unrealistic for them to expect greater change in their condition, not only because of their society's ambivalent attitude toward time-honored and male-oriented traditions, but also because of the fact that such traditions or biases cannot be modified radically even under more revolutionary conditions. A case in point is the historical experience of Soviet women who continue to express their frustration, rage, and grievances against discrimination and other abuses, despite the greater effort made in their society toward female emancipation and the elimination of gender difference.[45]

Second, the works surveyed attest to a more positive development in women's own perspective regarding feminist issues. Basically nonconformist in orientation and approach, Khuri, al-Samman, and Shaaban offer a perspective that is militant in tone and broad in scope. It has the salient characteristics of the Arab feminist movement in general: the rebellious (Khuri), the revolutionary (al-Samman), and the active feminist (Shaaban). These writers differ in their approaches, but they all agree in rejecting women's subordinate and cloistered position, just as they are united in advocating women's rights to education at all levels, work in different occupations, equality and independence in certain personal areas normally regulated by men: marriage, domestic responsibilities, and travel opportunities.

Finally, this perspective remains ambiguous at best, if not inconsistent when women's lifestyle, or male-female relationship, is addressed. Both Khuri and al-Samman seem to favor a drastic departure from the established norm of separation between the sexes, whereas Shaaban tends to avoid this highly sensitive issue at this stage of women's struggle. She seems to be more concerned with other fundamental rights that do not contravene the traditional code of morality or modesty as far as women's public conduct is concerned. There is a recurrent reference to the Western model of women's personal life, cited at times with respect and admiration, but ultimately rejected in favor of a new, yet-to-be-defined, Arab model based on Arab women's experience and their cultural values. Syrian women are advised to tread their own path rather than follow in

Western women's footsteps, for, as a Syrian woman declares, "there are good things in our culture which we should try hard to keep. We are capable of finding our own way without imitating the European woman in everything" (Shaaban). This notion, admirable for its emphasis on the positive elements in the tradition, remains, nonetheless, vague as to what extent women can deviate from traditional norms in their personal life.

SIX

Asad: Between Institutions and Autocracy

Patrick Seale

Most would say that Hafiz al-Asad, master of Syria since 1970, was an autocrat, an "oriental despot," differing only about the nature of the autocracy he runs. Is Asad simply the head of a junta of generals who might be compared with some Latin American military leaders of recent memory? Is he perhaps more like a party boss on East European lines, a variant of his friend, the former Bulgarian leader Todor Zhivkov? Or should he more properly be situated in the Arab tradition of the *za'im,* whose power derives from and is exercised through a network of patronage?

Some might prefer to say that Asad's regime is not like any of these models but should be seen as representing the triumph of a sectarian minority, the long-repressed Alawis, over their rivals in a Levantine society profoundly divided on ethnic and religious lines. In this argument, his rule, built on an accident of military power, can only be a freak of history, which must eventually give way to a system more representative of Syrian reality. This last model, of a Syria in thrall to an exploiting and dominant minority, is the one that hostile observers most often adduce to interpret Asad's Syria. Like all caricatures it reflects a measure of truth while — again like a caricature — overstressing a single trait at the expense of the whole. Certainly it is the interpretation that Asad resents most, considering it an unfair representation of the state system he has built. Indeed he has spent much of his adult life trying to escape from identification with his minority background, but the fact that his regime is still widely seen in these terms suggests he has been less than successful.

As in most societies, there is a difference in Syria between theory and practice, between the way power is supposed to be exercised and the way it actually is. On the one hand, there is in place quite an elaborate array of interlocking bodies and institutions that seem to have plenty to do; yet, on the other hand, towering above them is the intimidating figure of the president, olympian and unfettered, as convinced of his own rectitude and legitimacy as a Third World version of General de Gaulle.

Where does the reality of power lie between these two poles, between the institutions and the autocrat? The unexciting answer is that it probably lies somewhere in the middle: the institutions are not wholly sham and Asad is not wholly a dictator. When I last had an extended interview with him, in March 1988, I was struck by one of his remarks: "I have always been," he said, "a man of institutions." And, in explaining what he meant, he again evoked, as he often did in our conversations, his young manhood forty years earlier as a student politician in the Mediterranean port of Latakia.

In the late 1940s when Asad was still in his teens, he was an active member of the young Ba'th Party, fighting its battles in the streets against the Damascus government but also against the Ba'th's ideological rivals, the communists, pan-Syrians, and Muslim Brothers. He was elected chairman of his school students' committee and, in 1950–51, the year he took his baccalaureate, rose higher still to be elected chairman of the nationwide Union of Syrian Students.

What Asad remembers most vividly from those days, or at any rate what he chooses to remember, is the nature of student politics: elective, collective, democratic, idealistic. Students, he says, cannot be dictated to. They are natural democrats, almost anarchists. "I did not impose myself on those committees. The students elected me, and I earned their respect because I worked within their institutions." It is a common tendency to regard the past through rose-tinted spectacles, but it is interesting nonetheless that in Asad's mind there is an unbroken link between the student leader of the late 1940s and the ruler of Syria today. In his own perception—if not in that of many others—he rules by consent through institutions in which the people participate. Even in inner party counsels, he insists, the exercise of power is collective.

Very soon after he took power in 1970 Asad laid the foundations for most of the institutions of his state. They were not entirely his creation, for he inherited a good deal from his Ba'thist past—and primarily, of course, the party itself. He believed the party had become too narrowly-based, inward-looking and fanatical under his rival and predecessor, Salah Jadid. Asad wanted to open it up to the people. But whatever its shortcomings, it was then, as it remains today, the heart of his system.

But Asad's Ba'thist Party bears little resemblance to the party founded in the 1940s by Michel 'Aflaq (who died in June 1989) and Salah al-Din Bitar (who was assassinated in 1980), to the extent that a perennial subject of discussion among Syrian specialists is whether the differences are so great as to merit a new appellation for today's party, say, the neo–Ba'th. In shorthand terms, 'Aflaq's Ba'th was an opposition movement, whereas after the 1963 revolution, and even more so after Asad assumed presidential powers in 1970, the Ba'th became a party of government. Even though 'Aflaq once briefly held ministerial office and his colleague Bitar was repeatedly prime minister, their movement never truly crossed the line from opposition to government. For 'Aflaq, in particular, the party was a font of ideas, a mobilizing agent, a source of inspiration for the young. He preached that the backwardness and humiliation from which the Arabs suffered need not be permanent, but that one day Arab society could be reborn and become great once again.

'Aflaq saw his movement as a critique of government, closer to the people than to any regime. Indeed it was a dispute over the nature and role of the party that, after the 1963 revolution, set 'Aflaq against the young officers of the clandestine Military Committee founded by Salah Jadid, Hafiz al-Asad, and others in Cairo during the life of the United Arab Republic. 'Aflaq wanted to preserve the party's watchdog role over government, whereas they wanted it to be an instrument of government.

The experience of power over the last quarter of a century, and in particular during such great testing moments as the struggle with the Muslim Brothers, has given the Ba'thist Party confidence, even arrogance. The passage of time has regimented the party and made it less of a talking shop. It is no longer the heady, experimental, high-minded movement of 'Aflaq's time, but has become more of a bureaucracy, a power broker, and a source of influence and patronage. Any ambitious young man in Syria today would be ill-advised not to join it.

Is this party, whose reach extends to every corner of the country, simply the obedient tool of the president, or has it a life of its own? Can it be said to share, in any significant sense, in political leadership? Its organizational structure is well known. At the apex of the so-called Syrian region is a regional command of twenty-one members, of which Asad, as secretary, is the head. If there is one institution in Syria of which he can properly be said to be the head, it is this. It is probably the only body with which he meets regularly, as often as once a week, at moments of tension at home or abroad. He maintains, and there is some independent evidence for it, that discussions inside the command are relatively unbuttoned, that issues are decided by majority vote, and that even quite important matters can be settled by a majority of one vote, not necessarily his own. Asad claims that the leadership exercised by the party command is genuinely collective. Whether this is true or not, the party's very evident presence in Syria indicates that it has more than a cosmetic share in power.

What of party institutions lower down the pyramid: the party congresses, the party-controlled popular organizations, the party court, the party schools for cadres, and the command's executive bureaus, each supervising some aspect of national life? Does Asad dominate all these or do they have a measure of autonomy? His answer is that they have their own leaders and their own sphere of authority. "I am the head of the country," he told me. "I am not the head of every institution. Each has its own head."

The party's executive bureaus, for example, are quite powerful bodies, which are often in conflict with the ministries or state enterprises whose work they are supposed to supervise. The tendency on such occasions is for the bureau heads to appeal to the president to arbitrate in their favor. But, as Asad explained, he does not encourage such approaches, insisting that major quarrels, in particular, be brought before the full regional command.

Nor can Asad be said to be the head of the party-controlled popular organizations, corporatist structures created to define and control the main social categories of the Ba'thist state — peasants, workers, students, women, youth, and so forth. The men who run these organizations are genuine leaders within their own spheres. Of course they could not for one moment operate in opposition to the system. They are building blocks of the system, deriving their authority from it, but that authority is considerable.

Every four years or so, the party holds a regional congress, a great get-together, which can run for as long as two weeks, of some 770 delegates elected by the divisions, sections, and branches of the party's vertical command structure throughout the country. Reports are presented and discussed. By all accounts, these congresses are the prime occasion for rising Young Turks in the party to challenge their elders — but not of course the president — in a robust atmosphere of "party democracy." The sessions are not open to the public.

For the party, these congresses are of considerable importance. They put a stamp on a period; they may focus on a particularly pressing problem; they lay down policy guidelines for the years ahead; and they establish a sort of nationwide hierarchy of party members by electing from among their number a 90-man central committee, which in turn elects the regional command.

The central committee (which incidentally meets every three months for a day or two between congresses) is a body worth attention for the light it throws on the party elite at any given time. In addition to the twenty-one senior figures who form the regional command, the commit-

tee includes men and women on their way up the party ladder—party sec-
retaries at the gubernatorial level, provincial governors, generals in the
armed services and security agencies, ministers, members of the people's assembly, leading academics, heads of state enterprises, representatives of women's organizations. These are Syria's top people.

What of the other institutions of the state? Does Asad preside over
them? Once again, the answer is that he does not, that each has its own
head and sphere of responsibility. He is not the head of the government:
that is the prime minister. Nor is he the head of the people's assembly:
that is the speaker. Asad of course has a determining voice in appointing
these men. Chaired by Asad, the regional command chooses one of its
members to be prime minister and he, in turn, chooses the members of
his cabinet in consultation with the command.

Ministers are answerable singly and collectively to the people's assembly, a legislature first set up in 1971, when its 173 members were nom-
inated, before becoming elective in 1973. Although the Ba'th holds the
majority of seats, other political currents and groups are represented, as
well as a number of independents who form a sort of tolerated conservative opposition. Over the years the assembly was generally considered little more than a rubber stamp until, with presidential encouragement, it
surprised everyone in the fall of 1987 by directing sharp criticism at three
ministers and withdrawing its confidence from them. As a result, the government of Dr. 'Abd al-Ra'uf al-Kasm was brought down after seven
years in office. Since these events, the status of the assembly has notice-
ably improved, but it has some way to go before it could claim to be a genuine parliament.

If one were to visit a Syrian governorate, say Suwayda in the south or
Dayr al-Zur or Raqqa in the east, one might be expected to call on three
important personages: the governor, the party secretary, and the intelligence colonel in overall charge of security. One would probably discover
that these three men saw a good deal of each other, that they frequently
dined together and that, of the three, the party secretary was, at least officially, the most powerful. But the exact balance between them would depend on a great many factors—their personalities, their sectarian background, their access to the powers-that-be in Damascus, and on the
nature of the job being done in that particular governorate.

In a place like Dayr, close to the Iraqi frontier and with vulnerable oil
fields, the security job might be expected to have priority, and the colonel
would be correspondingly more important. In a fast-growing development area such as Raqqa, close to the Euphrates dam, the governor

would be the real center of authority, and this was certainly the case in the 1980s when the energetic Muhammad Salman was governor of Raqqa until his promotion to be minister of information in November 1987.

Governors are the senior representatives of the state in each of Syria's fourteen provinces, and may be compared to French préfets. In the exercise of their powers they are assisted by a structure of local government, which is an Asad innovation. Before him there was no local government to speak of, and everything, however trivial, had to be decided at the center. Beginning in 1972, a system of local government was introduced, which has been considerably refined since then, and which is probably the most nearly democratic of Syria's institutions.

The Aleppo governorate, for example — not just the city but the surrounding region as well — has a population approaching three million, or about a quarter of the country's total. It is subdivided into eight administrative areas, twenty-eight districts, and seventy-five municipalities. At the head of this structure is the governor, assisted by a 100-member governorate council elected by universal suffrage every five years.

The council has real powers at the local level, powers exercised on a day-to-day basis by the 10-member full-time executive board elected by the council to assist the governor. But the council operates under certain constraints. The first is that fifty-one of its one hundred members have to be "workers" or "peasants," giving these categories a built-in majority over the professional and business classes. A second constraint is that, in a country of centralized planning, Damascus has the last word on projects and budgets. Third, the governor and the council are watched over by a parallel party structure that is responsible for laying down broad lines of policy and for keeping an eye on implementation by the executive arm.

In the provinces one may observe the interaction of local government institutions with party bodies. The local party secretary is himself assisted by a 10-man board whose members have responsibilities — in health, education, finance, transport, and so forth — matching those of the governor's executive board. Thus party and government interact at every level.

Officially, Syria is not a one-party state and the Ba'th is not in a monopoly position. Although it is described as the "leading party," it sits with four other left-of-center political movements in a so-called National Progressive Front. In addition, Syria can boast of a number of political figures, mainly dissident Ba'thists, who have preferred to stay outside the front where, as members of insignificant splinter groups, they lead a precarious half-life on the margin of Syrian politics.

But such gestures toward political pluralism are of limited significance. Even accredited members of the National Progressive Front are not allowed to recruit followers in the army or at the university, both of which are exclusive preserves of the Ba'th. Nor do they have nationwide organizations to compare with that of the Ba'th. But they are not complete fictions either, seeing that they represent genuine and once powerful currents of opinion—Nasserist, socialist, communist, or dissident Ba'thist — which are now in eclipse but are allowed to survive in a vestigial form. Remnants of past political battles, these groups have more to do with Syria's political archaeology than with its current concerns.

It was, however, another of Asad's innovations to bring such enfeebled but like-minded parties onto the political scene. His predecessor, Salah Jadid, had been unwilling for the Ba'th to share the limelight with other political movements, but Asad argued that there was advantage for the party in giving public recognition to political currents, which had, after all, participated in the years of struggle leading to victory in 1963. In an evident search for a wider consensus, Asad appears to go out of his way in several of his speeches to mention the National Progressive Front, claiming to consult it and giving it an importance few Syrians believe it has.

The public tribute that Asad never fails to give to the institutions he has created is revelatory of something in his character: he is a man of order who values the concept of the state. Before he assumed power, Syria could not claim state institutions worthy of the name. The president, the council of ministers, the judiciary were at the mercy of a handful of all-powerful notables and ambitious soldiers. It is said that a cabinet minister's office was like a neighborhood coffeehouse where cronies dropped in at any time of the day to ask favors, usually exemption for themselves or their relatives from a law or a regulation. In contrast, Asad has introduced greater formality into public life. He wants people to believe in his institutions: the popular organizations, the people's assembly, the National Progressive Front, the local government bodies and, above all, the legitimacy of his own election to the presidency for three seven-year terms — so far. The backbone of the system is the party — the civilian party to mobilize, indoctrinate, and control the population, and the party in the army as the cure for the old malady of factionalism in the officer corps, in Asad's view the only real guarantee that Syria will not again fall prey to coups d'état of which, in his youth, he was a distinguished practitioner.

Surveying the various structures he has built, Asad likes to say, with a show of modesty: "I am *a* leader, not *the* leader," thereby explicitly challenging the view widely held in Syria and abroad that he is the font of all power.

What is the reality? Do the institutions of the Ba'thist state have any independent life, or are they mere camouflage for the personal exercise of power by the president? The modern state is Asad's creation, including the very institutions that he would like one to believe are autonomous. There is little doubt that he is Syria's master.

Among the reasons for his personal ascendancy is, first, the fact that he is the sole survivor of the small group of officers who from the late 1950s conspired to restore Ba'thist rule and who eventually seized power by coup d'état in 1963. His associates in power today are either friends from that period or else men who owe everything to him: he made them and he can, if he so wishes, break them. He is aware of it and so are they. His ascendancy over them, reinforced over the years, is such that he has achieved the status of an "elder brother" — a phrase he is fond of using to describe his position — who in a large family is treated with deference and looked to for guidance.

Another reason for Asad's authority is his record. He has weathered numerous storms and survived countless crises, with the result that his subjects and his colleagues in power have come to see him as a strategist of incomparable gifts. In the popular mind, he has been able to defy Israel, compel respect from the superpowers, defeat dangerous internal enemies such as the Muslim Brothers, and give Syria a regional and international stature it never enjoyed before. Asad's personal qualities of tenacity, caution, and foresight are much admired. It is doubtful whether anyone in the circle of men close to him believes he could do a better job.

Like any ruler anywhere, Asad needs men who will do his bidding and on whose loyalty he can depend. He needs instruments through which to exercise his authority. A score of men, the barons of the regime as it were, are of particular importance. He controls them and they control their own fiefs, and through these fiefs the country. Not only do they hold key jobs in the state — security chiefs, party bosses, divisional commanders — but through their contacts and alliances with the business community, they are among the most prominent members of a privileged new class many thousands strong. The relationship between Asad and his barons is not entirely one of master and servant. There are limits on how far he can push them, and the main limit is that if he were to get rid of them altogether, he would no doubt have difficulty finding substitutes as loyal, experienced, and able as they have proved to be over the years. In politics, as in other human endeavors, one has to make do with what one has.

The handling of these men, the balancing of one against the other, the way he promotes them in turn to his favor as if to head off any possible combination against him, is part of his secret of government. At one time or another, several of these men have attracted bitter, if sotto voce, criticisms from the public, because of their arbitrary behavior, seemingly ill-gotten gains, or lavish lifestyle. Asad's own tastes are somewhat austere, bordering even on the ascetic, yet he appears to tolerate excess in some of his closest associates. Is it that he is their prisoner and cannot discipline them? Or is it rather that, understanding the springs of human motivation, he exercises control over them in part by allowing them to enrich themselves and enjoy luxuries for centuries denied to the rural or small town communities from which most of them spring?

Asad's political leadership depends in considerable measure on his personal style. Yet, on the face of it, his public persona is not particularly appealing. He has always been formal and reserved, traits that the exercise of power have not eroded, without a gift for easy contact with people or the charisma and oratorical powers of a populist leader able to harangue the crowd. His style of public speaking is stilted, although his mastery of classical Arabic, considered the mark of a nationalist, is admired. Asad is probably cleverer than the late President Nasser of Egypt, the Arab leader with whom he best stands comparison, but he does not have Nasser's ability to move men's hearts.

Most leaders try to make themselves accessible, or at least to give the impression of accessibility. Asad's method is the very opposite. Not only is he extraordinarily inaccessible to even his closest colleagues, but he makes a practice of measuring out access to himself as if it were a precious commodity. He appears to have taken to heart Machiavelli's dictum that, in order to lead men, you must turn your back on them. Indeed access to the president is the name of the political game in Syria: those who have it, or can claim to have it, are in; those who have no access, however good their ideas or whatever their merits, must languish until he notices them.

At the start of his presidency, Asad was more gregarious than the solitary and reclusive figure he has become. He began his rule by a tour of the country, showing himself to the people, listening to their complaints and receiving their petitions. But over the years he has grown more remote—in part a result of the long trial of strength with the Muslim Brothers, when from 1977 to 1982 he was forced on security grounds to take precautions. He rarely makes public appearances except on carefully stage-managed occasions like the March 8 anniversary of the revolution, and it is striking that he has not been to Aleppo, for example, Syria's second city, for a dozen years or more. His subjects see him mainly on television.

At the beginning he used to govern, as most leaders do, by chairing committees and arbitrating between conflicting views. But now he seldom attends meetings except for those of the regional command. Even his ministers might see him only twice in their term of office, when being sworn in and on taking leave. He tends to have one-to-one discussions with his main colleagues—the prime minister, the foreign minister, Vice-President Khaddam, Chief of Staff Shihabi, Defense Minister Tlas—and even these discussions often take place on the telephone. Few if any of these men have the right to telephone him, a privilege enjoyed by only two or three of his security chiefs. He rings them, and functionaries further down the hierarchy, and he might do so at almost any hour of the day or night, for he keeps no set hours, sleeps little, never takes a holiday, and expects men in positions of responsibility to be available round the clock. To serve Asad is a daunting experience, and many a minister or senior functionary trembles when the president comes on the line. He expects them to be on top of their jobs and to have at their fingertips the facts or figures he may want. Woe to the man who gives him wrong information.

By such methods, as well as by his direct hold over his colleagues, he maintains unchallenged ascendancy. He has placed himself far above the rest of Syria's governing elite on a lofty eminence of his own, a position symbolized by the monumental new presidential palace that he is building on a peak overlooking the capital and which in 1989 was nearing completion. The distance between Asad and the others is underlined by the workings of a pervasive personality cult that inflates his image and deflates those of other men.

Yet, with all this, Asad in private contact remains courteous, humane with his associates, almost modest, an exemplar of morality and respectable family life, and the champion—perhaps the only one in the country—of legality and honest institutions. And it is this, too, that earns him the respect of his colleagues and sets him above them.

Talking to Asad, one cannot fail to observe that he has a lofty vision of Syria. He does not want to be seen as a dictator, still less as an Alawi revanchist or as the patron of an irresponsible and self-seeking "new class." He would like the Ba'th Party to be influential and lively, and he aspires to run a country of well-established institutions. But it must be said that his vision has not been realized, or at least not yet.

A first constraint is on social transformation. No doubt Asad would like workers and peasants, the social categories he came to power to defend, to play a bigger role in public life, a role commensurate with the improvement in their standard of living that he has brought about. But progress in this regard has been limited. One reason is that he has attempted to conciliate the merchants of Damascus and other cities because, for all the central planning and state ownership, the Syrian economy still depends heavily on the private sector. Businessmen may groan under state controls, complaining of public deficits, inflation, bureaucratic incompetence, and multiple exchange rates, but they continue to do well in Asad's Syria. There is no bias against wealth, and the predominant ethos of the people at the top is far from socialist.

A second constraint are the routine malpractices of the new class risen to prominence during Asad's presidency—the corruption, commission-taking on government contracts, black market dealings, evasions of customs, clientelism. Such profiteering makes nonsense of much state planning, prevents a fair distribution of wealth, and is an obstacle to growth and efficiency. From time to time Asad has tried to tighten up, but the corruption is so all-pervasive that a real cleanup is unlikely. The long, virtually uncontrollable mountain frontier with Lebanon, and Syria's military presence in that country, are no doubt factors contributing to smuggling and other abuses.

But the main constraint on Asad's vision of a respectable polity is the overriding and permanent concern for security: with some justice, Syria feels beleaguered, under pressure at home and abroad, not only from Israel and the West, but also from a variety of Arab opponents of which Iraq is paramount. Enemies abound. At home Asad feels he can afford no challenge, believing that a firm domestic base is crucial to the conduct of his often controversial external policy. This concern for security has caused Asad to run a more repressive system than he would like, and to rely on, perhaps more than he might like, his own Alawi community. It is strongly represented in the various intelligence agencies and security forces. For example, the colonels responsible for security in the governorates are almost invariably Alawi, as are the heads of the security services.

A casualty of the paramount need for security is that the ordinary citizen feels virtually defenseless vis-à-vis the state. However prosperous a man might be, or however eminent in his profession, he could be summoned for interrogation by one or another of the security organs, and, in the worst case, he could lose everything overnight. The notion of citizens' rights is not well developed, nor does the judiciary provide any real safeguard. In such a system, the only real protection lies in knowing someone inside the structure of power or close to it, who can intervene on one's behalf. This is the time-honored Arab recourse to *wasata,* which can loosely be described as a friendly hand from a person of influence.

Asad's regime is therefore one of paradox, his own personal brew of institutions and autocracy. How can such a system be judged or its effectiveness, popular support, and durability be gauged? And what can be said about the big question looming over all the others, that of the succession?

On the matter of participation, no one would pretend that Syria was a democracy or that the ordinary man in the street felt that he could change his fate, let alone the government, by voting in an election. The turnout at elections was generally low until citizens were required, in dealing with government departments, to produce proof of having voted. Pluralism cannot be said to flourish, in spite of the existence of the National Progressive Front.

But this apart, the Ba'thist state does seem to provide some opportunity for participation and a considerable number of Syrians appear to take advantage of it. Traveling around the country and meeting many a dedicated and enthusiastic party worker, it is less easy to dismiss the Ba'thist Party as a mere instrument of state control or a ladder for opportunists. A visitor to Syria in the early 1980s, for example, could not deny the fervor the party inspired when Ba'thists in arms were risking their lives in the struggle against the Islamic underground. One got the sense that they considered the state to be theirs and were ready to defend it. Indeed, had the party not been strong and its members not committed, it is doubtful whether the regime would have survived that ordeal. Asad won the contest, in Hama, Aleppo, and elsewhere, not only because he used force and great brutality to crush the uprising, but because the party stood firm. In these less critical times, support for the regime still seems to be genuine, as may be gauged by the enthusiasm shown at student meetings. These things cannot easily be faked. Everyone knew, for example, that Sadat of Egypt did not have the students on his side, whereas Asad largely does.

Like much of the Third World, Syria's population of about twelve million is overwhelmingly young. Asad has been there so long that he is truly a father figure to the half of the population under twenty. He fills the whole horizon. Anyone who has attended a congress of Syrian students, or events organized by the Union of Revolutionary Youth, one of the most important of the party-controlled popular organizations, which mobilizes youngsters between the ages of twelve and eighteen, cannot doubt that he is revered by the young. But whether this is participation or an expression of autocracy is not easy to say.

To Western tastes, the forms that participation takes in Syria seem overregimented, and the boundaries within which people can speak their minds seem narrowly drawn. For example, no one in Syria would be advised publicly to speak ill of the president, the army, or the Alawi community — all taboo subjects. As in General de Gaulle's France, foreign policy is a *domaine réservé* for the president. Whatever their private views, one hears no one in Syria publicly recommending a break with Iran, withdrawal from Lebanon, or endorsement of PLO Chairman Yasser Arafat's peace policy. It should be said that Asad's foreign policy has a wide measure of support among his countrymen. His opposition to separate deals between Israel and its neighbors, his insistence on a comprehensive settlement of the Arab-Israeli dispute to be reached at an international conference, and his determination to stand up to Israeli and US pressures are viewed with pride.

Ever since Asad fell ill in 1983, there has been considerable anxiety over the succession. Can the system function without him? Would his political line be defended as vigorously by someone else? Could a transfer of power be effected smoothly, without a destructive struggle among rival generals and without sectarian strife? These are not questions one can answer with any great confidence, but the events of 1983 – 84, when Asad's generals nearly came to blows in the wake of his illness, are not an encouraging precedent. Asad has not designated a successor and there is no crown prince in his regime. Because he is himself relatively young (b. October 1930) and because his health remains relatively good in spite of signs of fatigue, he may as yet see no need to organize for the future. Some observers believe his son Basil (b. March 1962) is being groomed for the succession by being given quite senior army commands — in the summer of 1989 there were rumors that he would soon be given command of a brigade — but he remains a young man with little political experience, and there is no evidence that Asad thinks dynastically.

What can be said, however, is that the political and security foundation of Asad's system — the Ba'thist Party and the Alawi community — are too firmly entrenched at every level of Syrian life, and most importantly in the armed services and the security agencies, to be easily shunted aside by a would-be putschist. Certainly there can be no return to the rule of city-based Sunni notables, which Asad's rural and small town revolution displaced. Any successor is likely to emerge from this background or at least to have the support of these new forces.

But having said this, few observers are confident that Asad's system is strong enough to survive his departure unscathed. He is the single most important unifying force in a country where many conflicts remain unresolved just below the surface, and, for some years at least, he would seem to be indispensable to Syria's stability. As one of his close associates put it to me with a touch of loyal hyperbole, "Asad is the only pole holding up the tent."

SEVEN

The Nature of the Soviet-Syrian
Link under Asad and under Gorbachev

Helena Cobban*

The Hafiz al-Asad regime that has ruled Syria since the end of 1970 has maintained a close relationship with the Soviet Union, albeit one that has often been marked by stormy disagreements. The present study will chart the dynamics of this relationship, which is one in which both sides seem always to be testing the limits of their independence from or influence over the other.

Alvin Rubinstein has defined "influence," in the context of the USSR relations with Third World states, as operating only through nonmilitary means. I would submit, in contrast, that in the context of Soviet-Syrian relations the "influence" of one side over the other can best be determined precisely in those circumstances where major decisions of peace or war are being made, when the primary instruments of influence are vested in the ability of one side—primarily, the Soviets—to offer or withhold military support to the other.[1]

Historical Overview

The initial agreement for Syrian purchase of Soviet arms was concluded in 1956, and the supply relationship continued in the years that followed despite Syria's frequent changes of regime and of regional alignment, and

*When she wrote this study, the author was an SSRC-MacArthur Fellow in International Security Studies. It should be noted that the bulk of the study was completed in September 1988. Its analysis foreshadowed to a considerable extent the changes in Soviet policy toward Syria that occurred in 1989, references to which were added in early 1990.

111

its defeat in the 1967 Middle East war. Until 1972, however, the Soviet relationship with Syria was always subordinate to that with Egypt: that year, in the aftermath of Egyptian President Anwar Sadat's abrupt ouster of seventeen thousand Soviet technicians from his country, the Soviets dramatically upgraded their relationship with Hafiz al-Asad's Syria (as they did also with the Palestine Liberation Organization, PLO). Soviet arms supplies during the following year allowed Syria (as Egypt) to launch the limited offensive against Israel of October 1973. Soviet behavior during that war, however, indicated that support of Syria's strategic aims was still not the Soviet prime goal in the area. Whereas the Syrians would have benefited from an early ceasefire, when their troops were still well forward of the prewar battlelines (though still short of the international frontier with Israel), the Soviets gave priority during the war to their relations with the United States and with Egypt. Thus, they did not push a forceful ceasefire resolution through the Security Council until October 22. By that time the Israelis had succeeded in pushing the Golan battle line well back toward Damascus.

In the aftermath of the 1973 fighting, Asad took a new tack that must have seriously worried his backers in Moscow. In May 1974 he responded affirmatively to US Secretary of State Henry Kissinger's efforts to follow up the disengagement agreement Kissinger had earlier brokered on the Israeli-Egyptian front, with a similar agreement on the Golan. Over the three or four years that followed, Asad seemed to be trying to reenact the strategy Egyptian President Gamal Abdel Nasser had pursued with some success in the late 1950s and early 1960s: maximizing his leverage with respect to both superpowers by playing them off against each other. Asad's successes in this ploy were more limited than Nasser's, however. He won some small benefits from the United States in the mid-1970s — endorsement of his move into Lebanon in 1976, small amounts of US economic aid, and the symbolically important prize of being able to hold a "summit-level" meeting with President Jimmy Carter in May 1977 without having to go to Washington to obtain it. The cost Asad paid throughout this period, however, was further erosion in such trust as he enjoyed in a Soviet bureaucracy, which had been deeply suspicious of his motives ever since he came to power in 1970.

Then, in late 1977, it was made extremely clear to Asad that there would be no place for him in the current round of American peacemaking efforts in the Middle East. This was accomplished when the Carter administration abandoned earlier efforts to reconvene a Mideast peace conference under UN auspices in favor of providing unilateral American backing to Sadat's dramatic peace overtures to Israel. In September 1978 this policy resulted in the conclusion of the US-sponsored peace accords between Israel and Egypt. Though the parties at Camp David invited other Arab states to conclude peace agreements with Israel along similar lines, insufficient inducements were offered to tempt any of them, including Syria, into the process. Indeed, Sadat had made it plain from the outset of his initiative that he wanted to act independently of any alliance or coalition with other Arab parties.

If Sadat's turn toward unilateralism in the Arab arena cut Syria out of the peacemaking process, then the US' analogous move at the international level had also cut the Soviets out of diplomatic action in the Middle East; it left them desperate to shore up what remained of their support there. The net effect of Carter's diplomacy on Soviet-Syrian relations was thus to drive the two sides back into each other's arms, notwithstanding the many reservations they still entertained about each other. As part of this rapprochement, the Soviets and Syrians concluded a formal Treaty of Friendship and Cooperation in October 1980, which committed the two sides to "enter without delay into contact with each other with a view to coordinating their positions" in the event of the emergence of "situations jeopardizing peace or security of one of the parties."[2] Soviet commentators were at pains to point out that this provision of the treaty did *not* apply in cases of threats to the Syrian troops still deployed in neighboring Lebanon.

US policy continued to have a great effect on the tenor of Soviet-Syrian relations under the early years of the Reagan administration. Reagan came into power accompanied by a secretary of state, Alexander Haig, who was committed to building an anti-Soviet "strategic consensus" between Israel and pro-Western Arab states. When this failed, he threw his weight into building strategic ties with Israel; and he gave what the Israelis understood to be an implicit "green light" to their June 1982 invasion of Lebanon.[3] During the invasion, the Israeli air force knocked out the Soviet-supplied air defense system that the Syrians had deployed in east Lebanon, and Israeli ground forces and attack helicopters engaged in several battles with Syrian armored forces.

This challenge to their major Mideastern ally came at a bad time for the Soviets, since they were then deeply embroiled in the power struggles engendered by Secretary General Leonid Brezhnev's long-drawn-out physical decline. Brezhnev, who had occupied his post since 1964, did not finally succumb to his illness until November 1982. Until that time, Soviet reactions to the rapidly moving events in the Middle East would seem minimal, cautious, and delayed (though there are indications that the decision to beef up Syria's own air defenses with SAM-5 missiles was taken before Brezhnev's final demise). While Syrian and Palestinian positions in Lebanon were coming under intensive attack from the Israelis from

June through August 1982, the Soviets gave them little help. Shortly after the Israeli destruction of the Syrian SAMs in the Bekaa, the Soviets did make a demarche to the US government, which was used by the United States in an attempt to rein in Israel—though one specialist who was in the White House at the time has admitted that the United States ''put its own spin'' on the Soviet message when it told the Israelis about it, in order to strengthen its impact on them. Another former White House official has said that satellite evidence of a mobilization of Soviet air defense troops in southern parts of the USSR accompanied transmittal of the public Soviet message.[4]

By late June 1982 it was clear that the Soviets had suffered a major loss of prestige in the Arab world because of their failure to provide more effective support to Syria (though the Arab countries were in a bad position to criticize, since they had not helped the Syrians at all either). The United States then emerged as the sole sponsor of the complicated cease-fire agreement in Lebanon to which the PLO and Syria were both parties —along with the governments of Israel and Lebanon, and several Lebanese militias. The United States thus seemed well placed to push the diplomatic initiative even further when President Reagan announced the launching of his own Middle East peace plan at the beginning of September 1982.

This peace plan notably made no mention of Syria's continuing grievance concerning Israel's 15-year occupation of the Golan Heights. From the middle of September onward the Syrians clearly were working to prevent the implmentation of this threatening new Pax Americana for the region. Their interest in this was shared, at the strategic level, by the Soviets. They later became even more wary of American intentions in Lebanon and throughout the region in mid-September, when the United States sent back to Beirut the Multi-National Force (MNF) units that had left there at the end of August, after supervising the PLO withdrawal from the city. Though the MNF's second deployment to Beirut was decided on for laudable, largely emotional, reasons, after revelation of the massacres committed by pro-Israeli militiamen in Beirut, the fact remains that the precise mission of MNF-2 was never clearly defined (as the Pentagon was to complain all along), and the Soviets feared from the beginning that it would be integrated into the US counter-Soviet strategic planning for the region. The net effect of the launching of the Reagan peace plan and of the MNF-2 deployment was that, once again, what the Soviets and Syrians perceived as American unilateralism in the region pushed the two wary partners back into each other's arms.

This time, Soviet-Syrian efforts to counter US plans for the region (both those that the United States actually harbored, and those the Soviets and Syrians imputed to them) were much more successful than the effort against the Camp David peace process had been in the late 1970s. In February and March 1984 the United States was forced to admit the failure of its peacemaking and peacekeeping efforts in Lebanon: MNF-2 was "redeployed offshore" in Reagan's memorable phrase, and Lebanese President Amin Gemayyel turned his back on the uncertain support of the United States in favor of a new relationship with Syria, abrogating the US-sponsored peace pact with Israel as he did so.[5] The Reagan plan for the region continued to sputter along as national US policy for two years thereafter, and received a further short lease on life when Israel's ruling Likud Bloc (which had firmly rejected the plan from the outset) was forced to share power with Labor after the elections of fall 1984. But by April 1986 the Reagan plan too was dead in the water: the last nail in its coffin was delivered when Jordan's King Hussein, now also entering a new relationship with Syria, declared he could not enter a peace process without Soviet and Syrian support.

What made these achievements of 1982 to 1986 even more impressive was that they were registered during a period when both Syria and the Soviet Union were undergoing periods of major uncertainty concerning their top leaders. In the Soviet Union, Brezhnev was succeeded as Secretary General by Yuri Andropov in November 1982; in February 1984 Andropov was succeeded by Konstantin Chernenko, who in his turn was succeeded by Mikhail Gorbachev in November 1985. In Syria, meanwhile, Hafiz al-Asad fell seriously ill at the end of 1983, spurring a deep succession crisis that did not seem to be resolved until the following summer.

The fact that, despite these deep domestic uncertainties, the Soviets and the Syrians could register such success in their counter-American efforts of 1982 to 1984 (both those they pursued in coordination with each other and those they pursued in parallel), would seem to indicate that these policies were backed by a significant consensus within the ruling elites of each country. It did *not* indicate, however, that they had erased the history of distrust between them. At the political level, the Soviets continued to be perturbed by some of Asad's other policies in the Middle East, particularly the single-mindedness with which he pursued his hostility to the PLO mainstream led by Yasser Arafat, which was supported by all the other Arab countries and by Moscow. The Syrians grew increasingly uneasy at the Soviet efforts, which accelerated under Gorbachev, to "reach out" to a broad spectrum of Arab states and even, albeit more tentatively, to Israel. At the military level, the Soviets did not at all want to be dragged into the kind of Arab-Israel confrontation to which they feared Asad's policy of achieving "strategic balance" with Israel might lead them. And at the ideological level, some parts of the Soviet influential International Department continued to express their deep distrust of the social value and political utility of too strong a reliance on Syria's Ba'thist regime.[6]

Thus was the scene set for the bombshell of April 1987, when Gorbachev invited Asad to Moscow, only to berate him in full public view at a state dinner, for the unrealistic nature of his policy toward Israel. Directly contradicting Asad's "strategic balance" policy, Gorbachev told him and the other high-level diners that "the stake on military power in settling the [Arab-Israeli] conflict has become completely discredited." He also warned Asad that he could not expect to be able to veto a future Soviet resumption of diplomatic ties with Israel, saying: "Let me put it straight: The absence of such relations cannot be considered normal."[7]

In Damascus, the Gorbachev speech seemed to provoke some rapid reconsideration as to whether or not the regime could continue to take Soviet diplomatic and military support for granted. Shortly after Asad left the Soviet Union, he withdrew his ambassador from Moscow in a move that seemed to signal discontent. A new ambassador was not sent back there until more than a year later.[8] On the Soviet side, meanwhile, one of the officials involved in drafting Gorbachev's speech later explained that the Soviet leader's aim had been "to get out of the rut of hoping that further military shipments would solve our problems with the Arabs." The official said that the Soviets hoped, with the speech, to stress the shift from military to political means of waging the Arab-Israeli struggle. He commented that the Syrians' ideal of "strategic parity" was "just another code word for the arms race," and asked, "anyway, how can we ever measure it?" Other analysts in Moscow had some fairly harsh judgments to make about the Syrians' ability to use the military hardware they already had to good effect.[9]

What did the Soviets' public 1987 demarche to Asad tell us about the evolution of Soviet-Syrian relations in the late 1980s? Some other signals of 1987 made its message seem ambiguous. Most importantly, in the summer of that year, the first of the MiG-29 fighter planes that the Syrians long had been awaiting turned up at Syrian air bases. Together with the SA-5 air defense missiles and the medium range SS-21 ground-to-ground missiles that the Soviets had sent to Syria in 1983, these planes would now give Syria a significantly enhanced military capability compared with the vulnerability it had experienced in 1982. (Israel's military capabilities had also been advancing in that period, of course.) With the exception of the MiG-29 delivery, however, the trend in Soviet arms sales to Syria in 1986–87 was characterized by a decline since the elevated levels of 1983–

84; and the periodic military maneuvers the Syrian armed forces had mounted since 1982, which had built up to division-level maneuvers in 1986, reportedly dropped off dramatically in the first half of 1987.[10]

Through the end of 1989, there still seemed to be a consensus among policy-makers in Moscow that the relationship with Syria was worth retaining, albeit in a possibly modified form. In November 1989 the Soviet ambassador in Damascus, Alexander Zotov, reportedly said that his country's efforts to meet Syria's future military needs would take into account Syria's "ability to pay," and observance of the principle of "reasonable defensive sufficiency."[11] After the publication of these comments, Zotov called a press conference to argue that his remarks had been quoted out of context. However, in an interview with a Kuwaiti newspaper at the beginning of 1990, deputy Foreign Minister Vladimir Polyakov echoed many of the same points Zotov had made. Polyakov did specifically note that "Syria is our closest ally in the region." But he also devoted a considerable proportion of the interview to arguing that:

> The Arabs must search for the quickest and best ways to settle the Middle East conflict, because if the conflict continues, tension in the region will increase and military arsenals will continue to be built up. . . . So far, the conflict in the region has not been resolved and certain Arab states are, regrettably, in a state of belligerence, and we take this matter into consideration. Therefore we use the theory of reasonable defense sufficiency. This theory must be used by all states and in all regions in the world.[12]

Clearly, therefore, the Soviets were undertaking some kind of a serious reappraisal of their commitments to Syria, parallel to though not necessarily of the same order as the reappraisals they were making and remaking to other allies such as those in Eastern Europe in those last tumultuous months of 1989. In order to explore the possible dimensions of the reappraisal toward Syria, it is necessary to examine the role each party to the Soviet-Syrian dyad plays in the strategic and political calculations of the other.

Syrian Calculations concerning the Soviet Union

Speaking to a March 1988 rally marking the 25th anniversary of the Ba'thists' seizure of power, President Asad defined his country's international alignment in the following terms:

> Our international relations are firmly within the framework of nonalignment and the Islamic countries. Our relations with socialist countries, especially the friendly Soviet Union, are growing. . . . The Soviet Union is always at our side in our struggle against aggression, and for the achievement of a just peace that restores all the occupied Arab territories and all the rights of the Palestinian Arab people.[13]

His first reference to the Soviet Union was greeted with applause from the gathered party faithful. But it was noteworthy that his reference to the socialist countries came only *after* that to the nonaligned and Islamic countries.

The Arab Socialist Ba'th (renaissance) Party had, since its origins in the 1940s, listed "socialism" as only the *last* of the three ideals vaunted in its trademark slogan (the preceding two being "liberty" and pan-Arab "unity"). Where commitment to "socialism," whether in the guise of local leftist parties or that of socialist or communist countries, conflicted with the Ba'thist view of pan-Arab interests, the Ba'thists had unfailingly put their commitment to pan-Arabism first. They had also always jealously guarded the freedom of international action that a nonaligned policy should allow. But in his March 1988 speech, Asad appeared to be placing his country's official alignment with socialism behind not only its "nonalignment," but behind its identification with the Islamic countries too. This new location could have marked a genuine shift in his beliefs (and in party ideology), or it could have represented merely a tactical accommodation with either his large Muslim domestic constituency or Muslim financial backers from the Gulf countries: either way, it provided an interesting insight into the wily Syrian leader's thinking at that time.

Syrian officials had taken care, during and after their forces' June 1982 defeats in Lebanon, not to join the public chorus of Arab voices that questioned Soviet commitments to the Arabs on that occasion. In an August 1983 interview with Western correspondents, Asad characterized his nation's relations with the Soviet Union as "strong relations of friendship and mutual respect." He added that "the USSR adopts an honest stand on the Arab-Israeli conflict. It works for peace and against invasion, occupation, aggression, and Israeli attempts to impose hegemony on the region's states. On this basis, the USSR has acquired our appreciation and respect." As though to underscore for his questioners that Syrian-Soviet ties were not ideological, he then immediately noted: "Had the US administration done the same thing, it would have acquired our appreciation."[14] Three months later, Asad assured an American journalist: "The USSR, in return for its fair stands on our side [at our side] against Israeli aggression and invasion, does not impose on us things which are connected with our internal or external affairs.''[15]

If the relationship with the Soviet Union could be described as non-ideological, then what concrete benefits did Asad and other Syrian leaders hope for from it in this period? The first clear answer to this, as reiterated again and again in speeches and interviews, was military help in order to stand up to Israel. That some substantial parts of the military backing needed by Damascus to achieve this were indeed forthcoming in the post-1982 period was detailed above. What, then, were the Syrians hoping to achieve with this backing?

In an interview in July 1987 Syrian Foreign Minister Farouk Sharaa underlined that Syria sought not military superiority over Israel, but strategic parity, or ''strategic balance.'' The achievement of this balance could help Syria achieve its aims either in the presence or in the absence of a peaceful settlement, he argued. ''If there is no peaceful settlement, then at least Syria should be strong enough to defend itself; or the balance could be positively employed in order to pressure the Israelis to accept peace in the region.'' He defined ''strategic balance'' as consisting of ''the sum total of the Israeli-Syrian balance with the commitments of the superpowers.'' Sharaa did not imply that this balance had yet been reached. He judged, however, that the Israel 1982 invasion of Lebanon ''had resulted in a serious setback for the Israeli strategy in the region, and strengthened the Syrian strategy in the region. It helped push the strategic balance more in Syria's favor, and it emphasized the importance of national resistance.''[16]

Sharaa was frank, though tactful, in this interview in admitting that there were areas of disagreement between his government and the Soviets. He tried to minimize the importance of the strictures Gorbachev had delivered at the Moscow dinner the previous April: ''When the Soviets speak of not wanting a military confrontation, it is because they think the Israelis *use* military confrontation. . . . We believe the Soviets would not accept any solution [to the Arab-Israeli dispute] less favorable than Syria's minimum requirements.'' Concerning signs of increased Soviet openings toward Israel, as also implied in Gorbachev's speech, Sharaa said the Soviets thought such moves would bring Israel closer to peace and away from a military confrontation. ''This is their view, not ours,'' he noted. Asked if there was any coordination between Syrian and Soviet strategies toward the PLO, Iraq, and other Arab countries, he replied categorically that ''We have our own strategy and they have theirs.''[17]

Regarding more precise details of the military commitments the Syrians sought from the Soviets, and of what they thought they had obtained from Moscow, matters are less clear. At the nuclear level, the Syrians were clearly concerned by the volume of the evidence that mounted in the 1970s pointing to Israel's possession of nuclear weapons capability.[18] In an interview in July 1987 Syrian Defense Minister Mustafa Tlas said that former Soviet Premier Aleksei Kosygin had assured the Syrians that if the Israelis used nuclear weapons against friends of the Soviets, then "the Soviets would respond."[19] (Other Arab strategic writers, such as Egypt's Mohamed Heikal, have pointed out that any Israeli introduction of overt nuclear posturing or use would be of immediate concern to *both* superpowers.)

At the level of conventional warfare, the kind of commitment the Syrians had from the Soviets became especially important during the June 1982 clashes with the Israelis in Lebanon (though the Soviets had always spelled out until then that their commitments to Syria did not cover any commitment to Syrian troop deployments in Lebanon), and then again as tension mounted between Syria and *the United States* in 1983–84. In November 1982 Asad himself stressed that "the Soviets are our friends. We ask them for weapons but we do not ask them for men and, therefore, we did not ask them today and we will never ask them to fight in our place."[20] The following March, his minister of culture, Najah al-Attar reportedly told the official daily *tishrin* that "the USSR would participate directly in combat at the edges of Damascus, if there were an Israeli attack."[21] Her statement, however, would have to be considered less authoritative than Asad's. For his part, when asked in September 1986 whether the Soviets would help the Syrians if *the United States* should attack Syria, Tlas answered that "we ourselves would answer such an attack. However, if US soldiers landed on our beaches, they should not forget that we have a friendship treaty with Moscow. We do not need Russian soldiers, only weapons."[22]

From Tlas in mid-1987, meanwhile, came a strong intimation that he felt the Soviet commitment to Syria at that time was less than what he thought it had been under Secretary General Andropov. "It is a pity we lost Andropov," he said. "It is a pity we have a weak Soviet power unwilling to stand up to the United States."[23] The Syrians' satisfaction with the commitment they thought they had from Andropov had been evident back in May 1983, when Eric Rouleau reported that Andropov had assured Asad at their first meeting that the Soviets "would not allow Syria to suffer another defeat."[24] Certainly, the evidence from arms transfers would seem to indicate that the Soviets' commitment to the Syrian strategic posture rose under Andropov, and then subsequently declined, since the Syrians received the SA-5s and SS-21s under Andropov, and then had to wait two years longer than they expected to receive MiG-29s from Gorbachev, who pointedly sent aircraft of this model to India and to Iraq before he shipped any to Syria.

At the economic level, the Syrians have not sought as deep a commitment from the Soviets as they have at the military level. Although one Western source estimated the Syrians' capital debt to the Soviets for major military items at $15 billion in 1987, other writers have pointed out that many of the Soviet arms transfers to Syria have been paid for on a cash basis by the gulf states.[25] The major Soviet economic project in Syria, as in Egypt, has been a dam project: in this case, the Tabqa dam on the Euphrates in northern Syria, which has contributed significantly to economic development in the area. Soviet and other East bloc states have also worked hard on upgrading Syrian infrastructure in areas such as road and rail transportation, which have a dual military and economic impact.

Since Asad first came to power in late 1970, however, he has tried to steer his country away from too close an economic relationship with the Soviet Union. The influx of petrodollars in the 1970s, both in the form of remittances from Syrian workers in the oil countries and from state-to-state aid from oil producers, allowed him to liberalize many parts of an economy that had previously been kept under stricter government control. In July 1987 his deputy Foreign Minister Diyaullah al-Fattal stated clearly that "our economic links in the region are with the West. We are not allies of the East." According to Syria's 1986 statistical abstract, the Soviet Union had been the largest source of Syria's imports that year; but the next three place on the list were occupied not by East-bloc states but by West Germany, France, and Italy.[26] Meanwhile, much of the exploitation of Syrian oil resources, which promised to make Syria a net exporter in 1988, was being carried out by joint venture companies run in collaboration with Western oil companies.[27]

Soviet Calculations concerning Syria

As noted above, Syria assumed increasing strategic importance for the Soviets throughout the 1970s, in almost directly inverse proportion to the decrease in Soviet influence in Egypt. Without a doubt, among the Arab states of the region, Egypt must count as the major strategic "prize" for any great power, both by virtue of its huge population and relatively large resource base, and because of its location astride the potentially strategic Suez Canal, with long coastlines on both the Mediterranean and the Red Sea sides of the canal.[28] Take Egypt out of the pro-Soviet orbit, as the United States was able to do during the 1970s, and Syria remained very much the Soviet strategic planners' second preference for an ally in the region. (If the Soviets considered for a while that Iraq could also help play this role, this became decreasingly the case once that country started to suffer the chronic attrition of its war with Iran, which left Syria as clearly the Soviets' number one strategic ally in the region.)

Why should the Soviets bother to have such an ally in this part of the world? For a long time, under Brezhnev and his foreign policy vicar Andrei Gromyko, this question seemed not even to be asked. After the Arabs' defeat of 1967, the Soviets seemed to feel themselves obliged to contribute to the rebuilding of the Egyptian and Syrian armed forces, which made possible the long-delayed counteroffensive against in Israel in 1973. Moreover, in the case of Egypt, the Soviets subscribed to the 1973 war effort even *despite* Sadat's peremptory treatment of their specialists just the year before. Then they saw him use the leverage he obtained from the war effort to parlay himself into an increasingly close relationship with the United States.

The intensity of the Soviet disillusionment over that experience with Egypt was evident in many of their theoreticians' later writings on the subject. Hints that it prompted fears concerning the reliability of other Arab actors, including Syria, have also surfaced from time to time in their literature. Certainly, in Syria's case, such fears might appear to be well founded, given the frequency with which Asad and his colleagues in the leadership refer to their willingness to entertain closer relations with the United States, provided only the United States adopt a more evenhanded attitude toward Israel.

The existence of such fears would seem to have militated against the Soviets becoming too closely entangled at a strategic level with any Arab ally after Egypt. Another factor acting in this direction would have been the very high risks inherent in entanglement in any full-scale military conflict in the Arab-Israeli theater. These risks have been amply demonstrated during the 1973 Mideast war, when Israel reportedly moved to the level of assembling and deploying its arsenal of nuclear-armed ballistic missiles. The United States, responding to reports of Soviet nuclear preparations, raised the alert status of its nuclear forces worldwide.[29] Notwithstanding these factors, however, the Soviet leadership did decide, after it received the final rebuff from Sadat in 1976, to continue upgrading its military links with Syria. Evidence for this decision lay in the leadership's arms transfer policy in the late 1970s, its conclusion of the treaty with Syria in 1980, and then the strong support it lent the Syrians from 1982 to 1984. What, then, was the reasoning behind these increases in the Soviet support of Syria, and are there any indications that this trend might change in the Gorbachev era?

Four major types of factors can be described, which might push the Soviets toward greater commitment to Syria:

— *Ideological* factors, including support of the Syrian Ba'thist commitments to secularism (against a possibly common Islamic threat), anti-imperialism, and state control of economic development.

— *Military* factors, which can be subdivided:
   —the contribution Syria's battlefield experience can make to Soviet understanding of front-line Western technology; and
   — the contribution Syrian and Syrian-based facilities can make to support the Soviet naval presence in the Mediterranean;
   — other strategic contributions Syria can make, especially by virtue of its proximity to NATO member Turkey.

— *Political* factors, including the following:
   —the straightforward value of having an alliance with a state that, on issues not of core concern to itself, supports the Soviet position in international forums;
   —the possibility that increased Soviet influence in Syria can be used as leverage in the Soviet Union's relationship with other states, including the United States;
   —the argument that Soviet "credibility" in the Middle East and throughout the Third World is on the line in Syria.

— *Economic* factors, especially given that a relatively high proportion of Syrian arms have been bought from the Soviets for hard cash.

The principal focus of the present inquiry lies in how these kinds of arguments may be affected by Gorbachev's "new thinking" in the Soviet Union.

At the level of *ideology,* there were many indications by the end of 1987 that these factors might become less important in the Third World under Gorbachev, and that in the case of Syria there was even a possibility that such factors might start to act against a closer Soviet commitment to the regime.

One of the benchmarks of Soviet foreign policy under Gorbachev became evident at the 27th Communist Party Congress, which met in February 1986. Whereas in previous congresses, the reports of Gorbachev's predecessors as secretary general had paid fulsome lip service to the contribution made to the anti-imperialist effort by the national liberation movements in the Third World, Gorbachev's report in 1986 barely mentioned the national liberation movements at all, dwelling at length instead on the need to shore up bilateral relationship with the United States.[30]

That this new definition of ideological priorities had strong policy implications became evident almost immediately, as Gorbachev made the concessions in the INF negotiations that were necessary to restart the whole arms control process with the United States, and then made the decision to pull out of Afghanistan. (By December 1987 Soviet Academician Yevgeniy Primakov was declaring baldly to a group of Westerners that the Soviets no longer always defined foreign policy in the ideological terms of "class interests," but recognized that "national interest" could sometimes be a stronger factor.[31]

Another key move made by Gorbachev in his early months in office was to restaff key areas of his foreign-policymaking apparatus. To head the Communist Party Central Committee's powerful International Department, he brought in Anatoly Dobrynin. Since Dobrynin had previously served many years as ambassador in Washington, this move seemed to emphasize the clear priority bilateral East-West factors would henceforth enjoy on the Soviet foreign policy agenda. Dobrynin's senior deputy at the International Department, however, would be a theoretician who had already played a powerful role in the department for a number of years, Karen Brutents, a specialist in Middle Eastern and other Third World affairs.

The role of Brutents is particularly significant for the present inquiry since he had published some very interesting work, dating back to the mid-1970s, which was surprisingly critical of Syria's Ba'thist rulers and Syrian officials, from an ideological standpoint. In a book published in English in 1977, for example, Brutents wrote that in some countries, ruled as he judged Syria to be by "revolutionary democrats," the state sector of the economy:

> Becomes the economic basis for the entire nationalist, anti-imperialist, and anti-capitalist policy of revolutionary democratic regimes. Not infrequently, it serves as an obstacle to the emergence or spread of private enterprise.
>
> This is quite clear in the example of the more developed countries such as, say, Syria. If there were not [state] sector, private industry and the entrepreneurial bourgeoisie would have developed rapidly here. Instances of corruption and self-enrichment by officials in the state sector do not negate this conclusion. This stratum, completely bourgeoisified in its psychology, gives itself over to parasitic consumption, but is as a rule not strong enough to use its illegally gotten wealth as a basis for major or often even for medium enterprise. Their socio-political role is another matter. In this respect, they are quite capable of acting as the potential basis for a pro-bourgeois policy.[32]

It is probably relevant to note that these criticisms were published openly at a stage when Soviet-Syrian relations were still passing through the problem period of the mid-1970s. In 1983, however, Soviet-Syrians relations had been much closer; but that year Brutents published another major theoretical work that was much more directly critical of the Syrian Ba'thists. He noted that in nearly all the countries in the "socialist-oriented" group to which Syria belonged, "today there are signs of a more distinct and often fully evolved right wing."[33] In these circumstances, the role of the pro-Moscow communist parties becomes especially important. In a chapter focusing on that role, Brutents devoted about eight pages to the strategy of the Syrian Communist Party, though he must have been well aware of the weakness of and fractiousness within that party. In 1972 the Syrian Party had entered into a "Patriotic National Front" with the Ba'thists, a move the Soviets had hoped would increase its power within the government, but which the Ba'thists had tried with much success to use to control and delegitimize the communists. In 1983, then, Brutents wrote that "the Syrian Communists do not close their eyes to shortcomings in the Front's activities and to the negative sides of the Baath Party's approach to cooperation with the Communists."[34] In an earlier chapter he had noted, as a general rule that would certainly seem applicable to the Syrian Ba'thists, that "unfortunately the revolutionary democrats themselves often turn cooperation with Communists into a mere formality. Moreover, their policy frequently tends to weaken Communist parties in one way or another."[35]

Brutents had thus written quite openly about the shortcomings of "revolutionary democrats" in general, and even of the Syrian Ba'thists in particular. The kind of correction he advocated in his theoretical writings, for a policy that he saw as relying too heavily on the revolutionary democrats and on the "socialist-oriented" states they ruled, lay not only in greater reliance on the role of the communist parties in those countries, but also in broadening Soviet contacts in the Third World to include more clear-cut overtures to "capitalist-oriented" states in the Third World, in a bid to maximize the contradictions between these states and the "imperialist" states.[36] In active pursuit of this latter policy, Brutents made a number of visits in the mid-1980s to "capitalist-oriented" states in the Middle East, including Morocco, Kuwait, Jordan, and—in January 1988 —to Asad's old nemesis, Egypt. In those states, this high-ranking ideologue of the Communist Party of the Soviet Union held what were generally described as "fruitful discussions" with such pro-Western leaders as Jordan's King Hussein and Egypt's President Hosni Mubarak. (It is noteworthy that he was also one of the listed attendees at the fateful April 1987 dinner in Moscow.)

In sum, then, by 1987 "ideology" seemed no longer to be pushing the

Soviets toward a closer relationship with the Syrian Ba'thists (even if it had ever done so, a fact which remains unproven.)

Concerning *military* factors, judgment concerning the extent to which they were operational in the early Gorbachev years seems more mixed. Without a doubt, the Soviets had learned highly useful lessons in the Israel-Syria fighting of 1982, concerning the capabilities of some of the NATO front-line conventional weapons. From the Israelis' counter-air and counter-air-defense effort in the Bekaa, the Soviets learned about the capabilities of such NATO systems as the F-16 fighter plane, the E-2C Hawkeye airborne warning and control system, Shrike, and precision-guided air-to-surface missiles, and Israel's own home-produced "drone aircraft."[37] From acquiring Israeli Merkava tanks captured by the Syrians, the Soviets were able to analyze its reactive armor, which might well have helped them in their development of an even more advanced type of reactive tank armor.[38]

The Soviets were able, moreover, to reap the benefit of learning these lessons with little compromise of their own front-line Warsaw Pact technology, since the Syrian troop deployments in the Bekaa lacked up-to-date and high-altitude air-defense cover, and the Israelis were unable to capture any T-72 tanks there. However, the Soviets' clear gain in being able to learn these lessons in June 1982 was offset by the loss in credibility they suffered in the region as a result of failing to provide the Syrians with higher-grade military technology at the time. This loss in Soviet credibility was mitigated only after their despatch of SA-5 air-defense missiles to Syria toward the end of 1982, a move that most American commentators have seen as raising the risk level to the Soviets in any future Syrian-Israeli engagement. The whole battlefield experience argument is thus at best a mixed blessing for a Soviet leadership, which, especially under Gorbachev, has become more vocal in warning that Third World conflicts carry an inherent risk of global escalation.[39]

Concerning the contribution Syria can make to sustaining the Soviet navy's posture in the eastern Mediterranean, this requirement was anyway less urgent with respect to Syria in the mid-1980s than it had been with respect to Egypt two decades earlier, for two major reasons. The first is that in the mid-60s, the eastern Mediterranean had had great value in Soviet strategic thinking, since it was an area from which American Submarine-Launched Ballistic Missiles could be launched against targets in the industrial southern regions of the USSR. The Soviet navy thus considered it an urgent task to be able to track the activities of US submarines and of the US Sixth Fleet in the area, and still required quite extensive shore-based facilities, including facilities for shore-based naval air cover, in order to achieve this. (Mike McGwire has even argued that the Soviets might have entrapped the Egyptians into the 1967 Mideast war in order to obtain the naval support facilities they needed there.) By the mid-1980s, however, a number of developments had lessened the Soviet requirement for naval support facilities in the eastern Mediterranean. The development of much longer-range submarine-launched missiles meant that the US navy could now launch these against the Odessa region from as far away as the Indian Ocean, giving it a much wider body of water in which to conceal its missiles. And the Soviet navy had developed a much greater capacity to operate for long periods away from port facilities. In 1987 or early 1988, meanwhile, as part of the Brutents-advocated opening toward Mubarak's Egypt, the Soviets once again started using Egyptian naval support facilities in Mersa Matruh, further lessening any reliance on Syrian facilities.

Concerning other strategic contributions Syria could make to the Soviet Union's posture, its ability to make such had probably not appreciably changed between the days of Brezhnev and those of Gorbachev. However, the Soviets' requirement for such contributions most probably decreased once Gorbachev had channeled the previous threat of global confrontation into a more stable bilateral relationship with the United States. Gorbachev's achievement would also seem to decrease the value of having a political alliance with a state like Syria that would routinely linc up to back the Soviet position on issues like Afghanistan or Central America, provided they were far enough away from home.

At the level of political leverage, particularly with respect to a United States that was increasingly the dominant focus of Soviet foreign policy, the link with Syria continued to bring benefits to the Soviets in Gorbachev's early years. For inclusion in the Middle East peace process was still, through the end of the 1980s, a clearly stated Soviet goal. It was the Syrians' ability to influence government policy in Jordan (and Lebanon, though that was less important) that in spring 1987 finally forced Secretary of State George Shultz to admit that the United States could no longer hope unilaterally to provide outside sponsorship for peacemaking efforts in the Arab-Israeli theater. However, it should also be noted that by 1987, the Soviets had their own increasingly strong direct links with Jordan's King Hussein, as they did too with an Egypt that was equally committed to bringing them into the peace process. So the value of the Syrians' role in this seemed to be decreasing.

And meanwhile Soviet strategic calculations changed so rapidly at the end of the 1980s that by 1990 it was possible to suppose that some Soviet policy-makers might start to judge that the Arab-Israeli *Pax Americana,* which they had opposed so consistently since the late 1960s, might now be the most effective guarantee they could obtain against the danger their public statements were increasingly pinpointing as the greatest threat the region posed to their own national security — that is, the spiraling acquisition by Israel and other Mideastern states of long-range missiles and unconventional warheads.

The Soviets' decision to cut their losses in Afghanistan boded ill in two ways for those Syrian officials who sought to maximize their country's value to the Soviets. Most importantly, it indicated that the Soviets now placed a much lower priority on the argument that they should maintain the credibility of their commitments in the Third World, regardless of the resulting cost.[40] And secondly, it erased the special value to the Soviets of maintaining a political alliance with Syria, which had staunchly supported the Soviet occupation of Afghanistan in international Islamic forums.

Summing up this survey of the factors that might push the Soviets toward greater commitment to the Syrians, then, it can be concluded that the trend in Gorbachev's early years appeared to result in an overall decrease in the benefits such a commitment would bring to Moscow. The trend seemed to be toward a spreading of the commitment (and the risk) that in the latter Brezhnev years had been largely concentrated in the link with Syria, between a number of different states in the region. Although these states still included Syria, their number also included such states as Egypt and Jordan, which remained funamentally pro-Western in their orientation, but could now offer the Soviets some concrete political benefits. This process of broadening commitments, it should be noted, was in some ways derivative from Gorbachev's basic overarching policy of pursuing détente in East-West relations, and from his insistence on subordinating all other foreign policy issues to this goal.

Conclusions

Ephraim Karsh has with some accuracy described the Soviet-Syrian relationship as "a mutually beneficial strategic interdependence between two allies, favouring each partner in accordance with the vicissitudes of regional and global affairs."[41] By the end of 1987, the vicissitudes of global affairs, in particular, had acted on the Soviet side to downgrade the importance of its ties with Syria.

One striking conclusion concerns the hard-nosed realism, not to say cynicism, that marks both parties to this relationship in their dealings with each other. Thus, while Asad did not hesitate to send his troops into Lebanon in 1976 when Premier Kosygin was still in Damascus, the Soviet Secretary General paid him back in spades eleven years later, in nose-thumbing terms, with his peroration at the Moscow dinner. By 1987 it seemed clear that neither side any longer had any illusions that its partner had very much ideologically in common with it. And each side seemed to understand clearly that it was, at best, the other's second or third choice as a strategic partner. For the Soviet Union's relations with Syria were highly dependent on its relations with the United States (as were Soviet relations with all third parties). They were also highly dependent on the state of Soviet relations with the strategic prize, Egypt, and also possibly with Israel. From the Syrian side, meanwhile, many in the Syrian ruling elite were frank about their preference for good relations with Western Europe, or the United States. But so long as Damasucs felt threatened by Israel, the Syrians were dependent on the kind of heavy weaponry that only the Soviets would supply. One implication of this for the Soviets is that if, through their own and Syria's efforts they succeed in convening an international conference that resolves the Syria-Israel conflict, then they will have little leverage left in Damascus.

This consideration of the interests involved on both sides in Syria's relationship with the Soviet Union would indicate that, precisely because on both sides the linkage is so dependent on actions and relations of third parties, there is considerable possibility for change as the Gorbachev era progresses. A continuation and upgrading of East-West detente, a deepening of Soviet relations with Egypt, and progress in Arab-Israeli peacemaking could all deeply affect this relationship.

NOTES

Introduction

1. Albert Hourani, *Syria and Lebanon: A Political Essay* (London: Oxford University Press, 1946), 6.

2. Ibid., 10.

3. Ibid., 14.

4. Acculturation as defined here is a distinctively different process than assimilation. Acculturation involves direct contact at both individual and group levels, is bidirectional, and is not contingent on a change of values. Assimilation, on the other hand, is unidirectional, requires positive orientation to the out-group, and identification with it. Therefore, assimilation involves a change in values. Hourani's use of the term, assimilation, above, is in fact acculturation according to the definition used here.

5. Carleton Coon, *Caravan: the Story of the Middle East* (New York: Holt, 1951. Even Coon, writing in 1951, admitted that the mosaic view of the Middle East was static and outdated, and failed to comprehend the changes introduced in the twentieth century by industry, parliaments, nationalism, and the revolution in transportation and communication systems. Although its salient weakness was its failure to explore the implications of social, political, and economic change, the strength of the mosaic view was and is its calling attention to the continuing ethnic diversity of the Middle East, including Syria, and its continued relevance for an understanding of politics as well as society and religion.

6. Alasdair Drysdale, "Regional Growth and Change in Syria since 1963," in *Politics and the Economy of Syria* (London: School of Oriental and African Studies, University of London Press, 1987), 64.

7. Ibid., 67.

8. Model here is used neither in an arithmetic nor mathematical sense, nor to indicate isomorphism. Rather, it simply indicates a broad framework of analysis with its particular attached assumptions.

9. Jacques Weulersse, *Paysan de Syrie et du Proche-Orient* (Paris: Gallimard, 1946), 86–88, 126.

10. Robert Redfield, *Peasant Society and Culture* (Chicago: University of Chicago Press, 1956), 112.

11. J. A. Allan, "Syria's Agricultural Options," in *Politics and the Economy of Syria* (London: School of Oriental and African Studies, University of London Press, 1987).

12. Norman N. Lewis, "Syria: Land and People," in *Politics and the Economy of Syria*.

13. Françoise Metral, "State and Peasants in Syria: A Local View of a Government Irrigation Project," in Nicholas Hopkins and Saad Eddin Ibrahim, eds., *Arab Society: Social Sciences Perspectives* (Cairo: University of Cairo Press, 1987).

14. Norman N. Lewis, *Nomads and Settlers in Syria and Jordan: 1800 – 1980* (Cambridge: Cambridge University Press, 1987).

15. Ibid.; and Elisabeth Longuenesse, "The Syrian Working Class Today," *MERIP Reports,* vol. 15, no. 6 (July – August 1985), 17 – 24.

16. Lewis, *Nomads and Settlers.*

17. Longuenesse, "Syrian Working Class Today," 21.

18. Hanna Batatu, "Some Observations on the Social Roots of Syria's Ruling Military Group and Causes for its Dominance," *The Middle East Journal,* vol. 35, no. 3 (Summer 1981), 331 – 34.

19. Yahya M. Sadowski, "Graft and the Ba'ath: Corruption and Control in Contemporary Syria," *Arab Studies Quarterly,* vol. 9 (Fall 1987), 422 – 61.

20. Alasdair Drysdale, "Ethnicity in Syrian Officer Corps," *Civilizations, vol. 29 (1979), 359 – 74.*

21. Clifford Geertz, "The New Integrative Revolution: Primordial Sentiments and Civil Politics in the New States," in Clifford Geertz, ed., *Old Societies and New States* (New York: Free Press of Glencoe, 1963).

22. Fuad Khuri, *Imams and Emirs: State Religion and Sect in Islam* (London: Saki Books, 1990), originally published in Arabic in 1988 as *imamat al-shahid wa imamat al-batal tanthim al-dini lada al-tawa'if wa al-aqiliyat fi al-álim al-ara bi* (Juni, Lebanon: University Publishing House, 1988).

23. Ibid.

24. Ibid.

25. Multiplex roles are those that cut across many interests and contexts. For instance, religious specialists would interact with their coreligionists not only in specifically religious contexts such as mosques, husayniyyas, or Sufi convents,

but also in tribal guest houses, village council meetings, or in markets, homes, battlefields, or schools. The interactions that cut across these contexts — political, economic, religious, kinship, educational—necessarily partake of all of them and are "multiplex" rather than instrumental, single-interest relationships.

Chapter 1. Syrian Political Culture

1. Albert Hourani, "Ottoman Reform and the Politics of Notables," in William R. Polk and Richard L. Chambers, eds., *Beginnings of Modernization in the Middle East: The Nineteenth Century,* (Chicago: University of Chicago Press, 1968); Ira M. Lapidus, *Muslim Cities in the Later Middle Ages* (Cambridge; Harvard University Press, 1967).

2. Albert Hourani, "Revolution in the Arab Middle East," in P. J. Vatikiotis, ed., *Revolution in the Middle East and Other Case Studies* (London: Allen and Unwin, 1972), 67.

3. The following discussion is based on Philip S. Khoury, *Urban Notables and Arab Nationalism: The Politics of Damascus, 1860–1920* (Cambridge: Cambridge University Press, 1983). Also see Linda Schatkowski Schilcher, *Families in Politics: Damascene Factions and Estates of the Eighteenth and Nineteenth Centuries* (Stuttgart: 1985).

4. Abdul-Karim Rafeq, "The Social and Economic Structure of Bab-al-Musalla (al-Midan), Damascus, 1825 – 1875," in George N. Atiyeh and Ibrahim M. Oweiss, eds., *Arab Civilization: Challenges and Responses* (Albany: SUNY, 1988).

5. Louis Chevalier, *Classes Laborieuses et Classes Dangereuses à Paris pendant la première moitié du XIX' Siècle* (Paris: Plon, 1958).

6. This is wonderfully illustrated in a recent study by Norman Lewis, *Nomads and Settlers in Syria and Jordan, 1800–1980* (Cambridge: Cambridge University Press, 1987).

7. See Peter Sluglett and Marion Farouq-Sluglett, "The Application of the 1858 Land Code in Greater Syria: Some Preliminary Observations," in Tarif Khalidi, ed., *Land Tenure and Social Transformation in the Middle East* (Beirut: American University of Beirut, 1984).

8. Hanna Batatu makes this point in the case of Iraq in "Class Analysis and Iraqi Society," *Arab Studies Quarterly* 1 (Summer 1979), 229–40.

9. C. Ernest Dawn, *From Ottomanism to Arabism: Essays on The Origins of Arab Nationalism* (Urbana: University of Illinois Press, 1973).

10. Although Arab nationalism was fundamentally a secular movement in which Muslim religious leaders took a back seat to Istanbul-educated notables,

there seems to have been a conflict within the Damascus religious establishment that paralleled the one that produced the Arab nationalist movement. In this case, the "have-nots" identified themselves with the radical reformist ideas of the *salafiyya* movement. Some of these ideas eventually contributed to the formation of the Syrian Muslim Brethren during World War II. On the rise of the *salafiyya* in Syria, see David Commins, "Religious Reformers and Arabists in Damascus, 1885-1914," in *International Journal of Middle East Studies* 18 (November 1986), 405-25.

11. Dawn, *From Ottomanism to Arabism*, and Khoury, *Urban Notables and Arab Nationalism*, support the contention that until 1918 the Arab nationalist movement attracted a minority; a dissenting opinion can be found in Rashid Khalidi, "Social Factors in the Rise of the Arab Movement in Syria," in Said Amir Arjomand, ed., *From Nationalism to Revolutionary Islam* (Albany: SUNY Press, 1984).

12. An extensive discussion of the rise of Arabism in Palestine can be found in Muhammad Y. Muslih, *The Origins of Palestinian Nationalism* (New York: Columbia University Press, 1988).

13. The following discussion is based on Philip S. Khoury, *Syria and the French Mandate: The Politics of Arab Nationalism, 1920 – 1945* (Princeton: Princeton University Press, 1987). Other assessments of French policy in Syria can be found in Albert Hourani, *Syria and Lebanon: A Political Essay* (London: Oxford University Press, 1946); S. H. Longrigg, *Syria and Lebanon Under French Mandate* (London: Oxford University Press, 1958); André Raymond, "La Syrie, du Royaume Arabe à l'Indépendance (1914–1946)," in André Raymond, ed., *La Syrie d'Aujourd'hui* (Paris: 1980); and Pierre Rondot, "L'expérience du Mandat français en Syrie et au Liban (1918–45), *Revue de Droit International Publique* 3 – 4 (1948), 387 – 409; Dhuqán Qarqūt, *Tatawwur al-haraka al-wataniyya fi suriyya, 1920–1939* (Beirut: 1975).

14. Albert Hourani makes this point in "Revolution in the Arab Middle East."

15. See Badr al-Din al-Siba'i, *Adwa' 'ala al-rasmal al-ajnabi fi suriyya 1850–1958* (Damascus, 1958).

16. See Edmund Burke III, "A Comparative View of French Native Policy in Morocco and Syria, 1912 – 1925," *Middle Eastern Studies* 9 (May 1973), 175 – 86.

17. This analysis is elaborated in Philip S. Khoury, "Syrian Urban Politics in Transition: The quarters of Damascus during the French Mandate," *International Journal of Middle East Studies* 16 (November 1984), 507 – 40.

18. On the rise of the Syrian labor movement, see 'Abdullah Hanna, *al-Haraka al-'ummaliyya fi suriyya wa lubnan 1900–1945* (Damascus: 1973).

19. Hourani, "Revolution in the Arab Middle East," 71.

20. Philip S. Khoury, "A Reinterpretation of the Origins and Aims of the Great Syrian Revolt, 1925 – 1927," in George N. Atiyeh and Ibrahim M. Oweiss, ed., *Arab Civilization: Challenges and Responses*. (Albany: SUNY Press, 1988).

21. See Hourani, "Revolution in the Arab Middle East"; Khoury, *Syria and the French Mandate,* chapter 23; Pierre Rondot, "Les mouvements nationalistes au Levant durant le Deuxième Guerre Mondiale (1939 – 1945)," in *La Guerre Méditerranée (1939 – 1945)* (Paris: 1971).

22. Hourani, "Revolution in the Arab Middle East," 71.

23. On the rise of the Syrian Communist Party, see Hanna Batatu, *The Old Social Classes and the Revolutionary Movements of Iraq* (Princeton: Princeton University Press, 1978), chapter 24. On the origins of the Muslim Brethren, see Batatu, "Syria's Muslim Brethren," *Merip Reports,* no. 110, 12 (November-December 1982), 12 – 20, 24. On the origins of the Ba'th Party, see Batatu, *The Old Social Classes,* chapter 38.

24. From Hourani, Foreword to Khoury, *Syria and the French Mandate*, xii.

25. Hanna Batatu, "Some Observations on the Social Roots of Syria's Ruling Military Group and the Causes of its Dominance, *Middle East Journal* 35 (Summer 1981), 337–38. An interesting, unpublished study of the Syrian military is Michael H. Van Dusen, "Intra- and Inter-Generational Conflict in the Syrian Army" (Ph.D. dissertation, Johns Hopkins University, 1971).

26. See Patrick Seale, *The Struggle for Syria: A Study of Post-War Arab Politics* (London: Oxford University Press, 1965).

27. Hourani, "Revolution in the Arab Middle East," 72.

28. See Batatu, "Some Observations on the Social Roots of Syria's Ruling Military Group."

Chapter 2. Class and State in Ba'thist Syria

1. Nikolas Van Dam, *The Struggle for Power in Syria: Sectarianism, Regionalism and Tribalism in Politics, 1961 – 1980* (London: Croom Helm, 1981).

2. Henry Clement Moore, "On Theory and Practice Among the Arabs," *World Politics* 24 (October 1974), 106 – 26.

3. Doreen Warriner, *Land Reform and Development in the Middle East* (London: Oxford University Press, 1962), and her *Land Reform and Development in the Middle East* (London: Oxford University Press, 1948).

4. Patrick Seale, *The Struggle for Syria* (London: Oxford University Press, 1965); Sami al-Jundi, *al-Ba'th* (Beirut: Dar al-Nahar, 1969); and Naji Allush, *al-Thawra wa al-Jamahir* (Beirut: Dar al-Talia, 1962).

5. Alleddin Saleh Hrieb, "The Influence of Sub-Regionalism (Rural Areas) on the Structure of Syrian Politics, 1920–73," (Ph.D. dissertation, Georgetown University).

6. Kemal S Abu Jaber, *The Arab Ba'th Socialist Party* (Syracuse: Syracuse University Pres, 1966); John Devlin, *The Ba'th Party: A History from its Origins to 1966* (Stanford: Hoover Institution Press, 1976); Ibrahim Salamah, *al-Ba'th min al-mudaris ila al-Thakanat* (Beirut: 1969); Jallal Sayyid, *Hizb al-Ba'th al-Arabi* (Beirut: Dar Al-Nahar, 1973); and Muta Safadi, *Hizb al-Ba'th* (Beirut: Dar al-Adab, 1964).

7. Raymond Hinnebusch, "Party and Peasant in Syria," *Cairo Papers in Social Science,* vol. 3, no. 1 (November 1979), and his "Rural Politics in Ba'thist Syria," *The Review of Politics,* vol. 44, no. 1 (January 1982a), 110–30; and Tabitha Petran, *Syria* (London: Ernest Benn, 1972).

8. Avarham Ben-Tzur, "What Is Arab Socialism," *New Outlook,* vol. 8, no. 5 (1965), 37–45; Michael Van Dusen, "Downfall of a Traditional Elite," in Frank Tachau, ed., *Political Elites and Political Development in the Middle East (Cambridge, Mass.: Schenkman/Wiley, 1975), 115–55; and Alasdair Drysdale, "The Syrian Political Elite, 1966–76: A Spatial and Social Analysis," Middle Eastern Studies,* vol. 17, no. 1 (1981), 3–30.

9. Raymond A. Hinnebusch, "Syria under the Ba'th: Social Ideology, Policy and Practice," in Laurence Michalak and Jeswald Salacuse, eds., *Social Legislation in the Contemporary Middle East* (Berkeley: University of California Press, 1986), 61–109.

10. Itamar Rabinovich, *Syria under the Ba'th 1963–66* (New York: Halstead Press, 1972); Munif Razzaz, *al-Tajriba al-Murra* (Beirut: Dar al-Ghandur, 1967); Martin Seymour, "The Dynamics of Power in Syria since the Break with Egypt," *Middle Eastern Studies,* 6 (1970); Gorden Torrey, "The Ba'th: Ideology and Practice," *Middle East Journal,* vol. 23, no. 4 (1969), and Van Dam, *Struggle for Power.*

11. Raymond Hinnebusch, "Syria Under the Ba'th: State Formation in a Fragmented Society," *Arab Studies Quarterly,* vol. 4, no. 3 (Summer 1982), 177–99; Ayad al-Qazzaz, "Political Order, Stability and Officers: A Comparative Study of Iraq, Syria and Egypt from Independence to June 1967," *Middle East Forum* (November 1963), and Hinnebusch, "Syria under the Ba'th."

12. Petran, *Syria,* and Hinnebusch, "Syria under the Ba'th."

13. Avraham Ben-Tzur, "What Is Arab Socialism," *New Outlook,* vol. 8, no. 5 (1965), 37–45; and Hinnebusch, "Syria under the Ba'th."

14. Malikah Abyad, "Values of Syrian Youth: A Study Based on Syrian Students in Damascus University" (M.A. thesis, American University in Beirut, 1968).

15. Alisdair Drysdale, "The Regional Equalization of Health Care and Education in Syria Since the Ba'thi Revolution," *International Journal of Middle East Studies*, vol. 13 (1987). 93–111; and Harold Lemel, "Rural Social Services," in USAID, *Syria: Agricultural Sector Assessment*, vol. 5 (Washington, D.C.: 1980.

16. Syrian Arab Republic (SAR), *Statistical Abstract 1984* (Damascus: Central Bureau of Statistics, 1984), 88, 94.

17. Syrian Arab Republic (SAR), *1970–71 Agricultural Census Data: First Stage Basic Data in Syrian Arab Republic* (Damascus: Central Bureau of Statistics, 1970–71); Syrian Arab Republic (SAR) *Census Data: Second Stage, Detailed Data* (Damascus: Central Bureau of Statistics, 1971); Syrian Arab Republic (SAR) *Neshrat al-Ihsa'iya Sanawi lil-Qita al-Ta'awuni [Annual statistical bulletin of the cooperative sector]* (Damascus: Ministry of Agriculture, 1972); and Syrian Arab Republic (SAR), *Statistical Abstract, 1984* (Damascus: Central Bureau of Statistics, 1984).

18. Elizabeth Longuenesse, "The Class Nature of the State in Syria," *MERIP Reports*, vol. 9, no. 4 (1979), 3–11; and World Bank, *Syrian Arab Republic: Development Prospects and Policies*, vol. 2 (1980), 90.

19. Elizabeth Longuenesse, "La Classe Ouvrière au Proche Orient: La Syrie," *Pensée*, no. 197 (February 1978), 120–32; and Françoise Metral, "Le Monde Rural Syrien a l'Ere des Réformes (1958–1978)," in André Raymond et al., *La Syrie d'Aujourd'hui* (Paris: GNRS, 1980), 68–89.

20. Hanna Batatu, "Some Observations on the Social Roots of Syria's Ruling Military Group and the Causes of its Dominance," *Middle East Journal*, vol. 35, no. 3 (Summer 1981); Jean Leca, "Social Structure and Political Stability: Comparative Evidence from the Algerian, Syrian, and Iraqi Cases," in Adeed Dawisha and I. William Zartman, eds., *Beyond Coercion: The Durability of the Arab State* (London: Croom Helm, 1988), 164–202; Moshe Maoz, "Syria under Hafiz al-Asad: A Political Profile," *Jerusalem Quarterly* 8 (1978); Yahya Sadowski, "Cadres, Guns, and Money: The Eighth Regional Congress of the Syrian Ba'th," *MERIP Reports*, vol. 15, no. 6 (July–August 1985); Adeed Dawisha, "Syria Under Asad, 1970–78: The Centres of Power," *Government and Opposition*, vol. 13, no. 3 (Summer 1978); and Moshe Maoz, "Syria under Hafiz al-Asad: New Domestic and Foreign Policies," in *Jerusalem Papers on Peace Problems* (1975).

21. Elizabeth Picard, "Clans militaires et pouvoir ba'thiste en Syrie," *Orient* (Hamburg, 1979), 49–62, and her, "Ouverture économique et renforcement militaire en Syrie," *Oriente Moderne*, vol. 59, nos. 7–12 (1979), 663–76.

22. Raymond Hinnebusch, "Syria," in Shireen Hunter, ed., *The Politics of Islamic Revivalism* (Bloomington: Indiana University Press, 1988), 39–55.

Chapter 3. The Alawis of Syria

1. Abdul-Karim Zaydan, *The Individual and the State in Islamic Law* (Baghdad: Dar Salman al-A'zami, 1965), 18, in Arabic.

2. H. Lammens, *Les Nosairis, Notes sur leur Histoire et leur Religion,* Etude, no. 16 (1989), 461–94; and Hashim Uthman, *The Alawis between Myth and Reality* (Beirut: Mu'assassat al-A'lami, 1980), 112, in Arabic.

3. Ali Aziz Ibrahim al-Alawi, *Alawis the Unknown Shi'a Martyrs* (Damascus: 1972), 194, in Arabic; and Uthman, *Alawis between Myth and Reality,* 118–20.

4. R. Dussaud, in E. Bouillon, ed., *Histoire et Religion des Nosairis* (Paris: 1900); Lammens, *Les Nosairis;* and Mohammad Amin Ghaleb al-Tawil, *The History of the Alawis* (Beirut: Dar al-Andalus, 1966):97, in Arabic.

5. Read for an illustration the works of R. Dussaud, *Histoire et Religion des Nosairis;* H. Lammens, *Les Nosairis;* and C. Nieger, "Choix de Documents sur le Territoire des Alaouites," in *Revue du Monde Musulmans* 44 (March 1922), 57–68.

6. *The Book of Synthesis* was first published in 1864 in Beirut by Sulaiman Effendi in a volume titled *al-Bakura al-Salmaniya.* The book was translated into English by Salisbury. Some parts of *The Messages of Wisdom* are available in the Oriental Room of the British Museum.

7. al-Tawil, *History of the Alawis,* 203.

8. Ibid., 199.

9. Ibid., 197.

10. al-Alawi, *Alawis the Unknown Shi'a Martyrs,* 227–31.

11. *The Great Guidance* (al-Hidaya al-Kubra), written by al-Khusaibi, is one of the most cherished religious books among the Alawis. It discusses these issues in great detail. Unfortunately, I was unable to locate it anywhere in Lebanon or Syria, or in many well-known libraries of the West.

12. al-Tawil, *History of the Alawis,* 183.

13. The Alawis add Sulaiman al-Farsi according to a *hadith* related to the Prophet saying: "Sulaiman is from us, we the People of the House." See also al-Tawil, *History of the Alawis,* 182.

14. The *Ithna 'Ashariyya* (Twelver) sect of Islam is the dominant religious group in Iran and South Lebanon. The Ismaili sect of Islam (whose head is the Agha Khan) has large numbers in India, Pakistan, and East Africa. See also Munir al-Sharif, *The Alawi Muslims* (Damascus: Dar al-Umumiya, 1961), in Arabic.

15. See *al-Nahda* journal for 1938, July issue.

16. al-Tawil, *History of the Alawis,* 75.

17. Ibid., 76.

18. Ibid., 183.

19. Ibid., 77.

20. Ibid., 201–02 for more details.

21. Dussaud, *Histoire et Religion des Nosairis,* 166–79.

22. al-Tawil, *History of the Alawis,* 275.

23. See al-Alawi, *Alawis the Unknown Shi'a Martyrs,* for details.

24. Ibid., 177, 207–215.

25. al-Tawil, *History of the Alawis,* 477.

26. The Qamariyun today are headed by Sheikh Sulaiman al-Ahmad who carries the title "the servant of the People of the House"; he lived in Qirdaha village, the same village from which President Asad of Syria comes.

27. Hana Batatu, "Some Observations on the Social Roots of Syria's Ruling Military Group and the Causes of its Dominance," *Middle East Journal* 35 (1981), 335.

Chapter 4.   Land Reform and Class Structure in Rural Syria

1. One may ask why and how a family from Aleppo, two hundred kilometers to the west, came to own land along the Euphrates. Such an isolated fact can be located within a larger historico-economic phenomenon that emerged at the turn of the century, and even back into the nineteenth century. As a result of mercantile European colonial penetration while it was still under Ottoman domination, Syria came to lose its former trading role and subsequently experienced a process of social regression. The trading role of Syrian towns was henceforth trivial, since they served only the Mesopotamian and Arabian hinterland. The ruining of craft industries through competition with European imports aggravated the crisis. It was then, as Samir Amin states:

That in order to survive, the urban ruling class of Syria "feudalized" themselves, that is, endeavored to obtain from the peasants of western Syria the surplus they could no longer obtain from trade. The formation of the latifundia goes back to the nineteenth century, when the mercantile bourgeoisie, which had lost its function, began to turn to the countryside.

See S. Amin, *Unequal Development—An Essay on the Social Formations of Peripheral Capitalism,* translated by Brian Pearce (New York: Monthly Review Press, 1976), 309.

2. In the early stages they were not capable of exploiting all the land. The land needed leveling and general repair. In the early 1950s they cultivated only seventy hectares. In 1954–1955 they purchased two tractors and other modern machinery. By 1960 they were cultivating all the land of their village, an area exceeding 400 hectares.

3. A *khan* is a caravansaray, a storehouse, an inn, a hostel, a tavern, and also a place or center for trade and market activity. In the local idiom, a *khanji* is a *khan* keeper. In traditional medieval Islamic cities, *khans* were not only big storehouses with impressive gates and structures, but were also places where most goods were traded. In modern times a *khanji* was simply a merchant and a moneylender. Usually in the structure of his *khan,* always located in the old sections of large cities, he would have his office(s), which were staffed by one or two accountants.

4. O'Laughlin defines social formations as "rational systems composed of superstructure and a determinant economic base which may itself be a complex articulation of more than a single mode of production." For Hindess and Hirst, "social formation may loosely be said to correspond to the ideological notion of society. It designates a complex structure of social relations, a unity of economic, ideological, and in certain cases, political structural levels in which the role of the economy is determinant" (1976), 16. See B. O'Laughlin, "Marxist Approaches in Anthropology," in J. Siegel, ed., *Annual Review of Anthropology,* vol. 4 (1975), 341–70; and B. Hindess and P. Hirst, *Precapitalist Modes of Production* (London: Routledge & Keegan Paul, 1975).

5. As for the conditions of peasants in Syria in general, Rifat al-Asad maintained that the *fellah* was subjected to a merciless form of exploitation, whether in capitalist farming or in traditional farming controlled by feudal relations of production. The Syrian *fellahin* have called for the formulation of a law that will secure for them protection from feudal greed and exploitation, at least so they will not be forced off the land. The *fellahin* struggled for a long time to secure such a law, but the parliament stood against them in 1955 and refused to pass it. Only in 1957, after the "progressive forces" had exercised tremendous pressure (in parliament), was this law passed. See R. al-Asad, *The Economic Social and Political Development in the Syrian Arab Region Between the National Revolution and the*

Class Revolution 1946–1963, in Arabic (Damascus: Ad-Dar Al-Wataniyyah Distributions, 1973), 45–46. Over 50 percent of the land under cultivation was owned by 2,733 proprietors, while 600,000 peasants shared less than 13 percent of the land (1978). See sources cited in Y. Sadowski, "The Knife's Edge: A study of the Failure of Liberalization in Syria," unpublished seminar paper (Los Angeles: University of California at Los Angeles, 1978).

6. P. Bourdieu, *Outline of a Theory of Practice,* translated from French by Richard Nice (Cambridge: Cambridge University Press, 1977), 172.

7. Ibid., 179.

8. I personally recall the time when my father, among many others, volunteered to work in the election campaign of 1961 for Sheikh Faisal al-Haweidi. For some weeks when he came home in Ar Raqqa, he emptied his pockets of small brown bags, which were stuffed with identity cards of various people from different villages. Since he did not read or write, he used to ask me to classify and make lists of all those identity cards they had purchased and had kept with them so as to guarantee they be cast for Sheikh Faisal's ballot.

9. T. Apter, ed., "Political Religion in the New Nations," in Clifford Geertz, ed., *Old Societies and New States,* (New York: Free Press of Glencoe, 1963), 57–105.

10. Social scientists view the political process of mobilization for the consolidation of the Ba'th socialist system in terms of three successive phases: (1) 1963–66, (2) 1966–70, (3) 1970 to the present. In each of these phases, the party/state practice and ideological orientation for mobilization is modified so as to tighten or broaden its base of legitimacy and support.

11. H. Batatu, "Some Observations on the Social Roots of Syria's Ruling Military Group and the Causes for its Dominance," *Middle East Journal,* vol. 35, no. 3 (Summer 1981), 331–44.

12. Following the secession of Syria from the UAR (September 28, 1961), the new (old) regime, wasting no time, drastically modified Law no. 161 with Law no. 3 (February 20, 1962). However, in March 1963, following a successful coup d'état, which dislodged the government from power, Law no. 2 (March 2, 1963) was enacted, a remodification. Still, in 1963, important changes were added to Law no. 161, decreasing the maximum allowed limit of agricultural land from 80 hectares in irrigated land to 40 hectares and from 300 hectares in rain-fed land to 80 to 140 hectares depending on the rainfall zone. See S. M. Kaylani, "The Role of Agriculture in the Development of Syria, 1945–1960" (M. A. thesis, American University of Beirut, 1964), 44.

13. This general state of affairs is very well expressed in a petition this new social class presented to President Hafiz al-Asad, after the success of what we referred to as *al haraka al-tashihiya* (the corrective movement of November

1970). In the petition, they describe their state of "oppression, degradation, and alienation" under the Jadid-Atassi regime. Below only short excerpts of a long petition are translated so as to convey the way they described their own perception of their condition and also their optimism for better prospects under the new leadership. It reads:

> We, the delegation of Muhafazat Ar Raqqa are honored to present the following:
> . . . . The new declaration by the Provisional President Regional Command came like a cool breeze onto the fire that has been burning in our breasts, and it created refreshing breezes of hope which embraced every hill in this Arab region. The people welcomed the first steps of this blessed movement and this has been shown by their joining ranks which are marshaled toward unity. Since we are the representatives of segments of these good people, and because our great trust is in those who trust in God, and the goodness of men, and to those who faithfully try to reform what had been corrupted by the period of "oppression and deviation," we present to you with greetings of appreciation and gratitude our complaints regarding some areas of malaise that remain, hoping that the free people will take the initiative in their remedy and treatment. . . .

> The period of "oppression and deviation" murdered all manifestations and aspects of freedom and dignity. It desired to erase these words from the dictionaries of the language. Thus the first cries which rang out from the masses as they welcomed the blessed movement: "give us our portion of freedom, dignity, and honor."

14. G. Salame, *State and Society in the Arab East,* in Arabic (Beirut: Center of Arab Unity Studies, 1987), 191.

15. R. Hinnebusch, "Rural Politics in Ba'thist Syria: A Case Study of the Role of the Countryside in the Political Development of Arab Socialism," in Saad Eddin Ibrahim and Nicholas Hopkins, eds., *Arab Society in Transition* Cairo: American University in Cairo Press, 1977), 290.

16. Sadowski, "The Knife's Edge."

17. T. Petran, *Syria* (New York: Praeger Publishers, 1972).

18. A. Rabo, *Change on the Euphrates* (Stockholm: Studies in Social Anthropology, 1986), 153; and Hinnebusch, "Rural Politics in Ba'thist Syria."

Chapter 5. The Emancipation of Women in Contemporary Syrian Literature

1. Nabil Sulayman, *al-niswiyya fi al-kitab al-suri al-madrasi 1967 – 1976* (Damascus: Ministry of Culture, 1978), 41–49.

2. Ibid., 79–134.

3. *al-mar'a al-arabiyya al-suriyya fi aqd al-mar'a al-dawli: 1975 – 1985,* Union of the Syrian Women (Damascus: Regional Command Press, 1987), 217.

4. Ibid., 10.

5. Muhammad S. al-Akhras, *tarkib al-a'ila al-arabiyya wa waza'ifuha* (Damascus: Ministry of Culture, 1976), 226 – 29. The author states that he devoted several years to his fieldwork, but he does not indicate the year or period covered. We are informed, however, that before and after receiving his Ph.D. in sociology from the University of California, Berkeley, in 1969, he had done and is doing sociological fieldwork, including the sociology of the family. See his *Revolutionary Change and Modernization in the Arab World* (Damascus, 1972).

6. Nadia Hijab, *Womenpower: the Arab Debate on Women at Work* (Cambridge and New York: Cambridge University Press, 1988), 7.

7. Ibid., 3.

8. Bouthaina Shaaban, *Both Right and Left Handed: Arab Women Talk About Their Lives* (London: Women's Press, 1988), 236.

9. Yvonne Y. Haddad, "Traditional Affirmations Concerning the Role of Women as Found in Contemporary Arab Islamic Literature," in June I. Smith, ed., *Women in Contemporary Muslim Societies* (London: Associated Press, and Lewisburg: Bucknell University Press, 1980), 68–69.

10. Salih J. Altoma, "Sociopolitical Themes in the Contemporary Arabic Novel: 1950 – 1970," in H. E. Lewald, ed., *The Cry of Home: Cultural Nationalism and the Modern Writer* (Knoxville: University of Tennessee Press, 1972), 351 – 73); Halim Barakat, "The Arab Family and the Challenge of Social Transformation," in Elizabeth W. Fernea, ed., *Women and the Family in the Middle East: New Voices of Change* (Austin: University of Texas Press, 1985), 27 – 48; Miriam Cooke, "Telling their Lives: A Hundred Years of Arab Women's Writings," *World Literature Today* 60 (1986): 212 – 16; and Rose Ghorayeb, "Arab Feminine Literature Between 1850 and 1950," *Al-Raida* 7 (May 1985): 4 – 5.

11. Kulit al-Khuri, *ayyam ma'ah* (Beirut: Dar al-Kutub, 1959); idem, *layla wahida* (Beirut: al-Maktabal al-Tijari, 1961); idem, *wa marra sayf* (Damascus: Union of Arab Writers, 1975).

12. al-Khuri, *ayyam ma'ah,* 22–31.

13. Ibid., 56–57.

14. al-Khuri, *layla wahida,* 26–27.

15. Ibid., 27.

16. Tarif Khalidi, "Toccata and Fugue," *Middle East Forum* 37 (October 8, 1961), 24.

17. Husam al-Khatib, "hawl al-riwaya al-nisa'iyya fi suriyya," *al-ma'rifa,* no. 167 (February 1976): 50.

18. Evelyne Accad, *Veil of Shame: The Role of Women in the Contemporary Fiction of North Africa and the Arab World* (Sherbrook, Quebec: Naaman, 1978), 110.

19. al-Khuri, *wa marra sayf,* 89–90.

20. Ibid., 239.

21. Ibid., 192–95.

22. Nadia Youssef, "The Status and Fertility Patterns of Muslim Women," in Lois Beck and Nikki Keddie, eds., *Women in the Muslim World* (Cambridge: Harvard University Press, 1978), 80.

23. Ghali Shukri, *Ghadah al-Samman bila ajniha* (Beirut: Dar al-Tali'ah, 1977), 42.

24. Ghadah al-Samman, *'Aynak Qadari,* (Beirut: al-Adab 1962), 8–20, 46–64, 144–50.

25. Ibid., 90–99.

26. Ibid., 98–99.

27. Hanan Ahmad Awwad, *Arab Causes in the Fiction of Ghadah al-Samman (1961–1975)* (Sherbrook, Quebec: Naaman, 1983), esp. 53–74.

28. Shukri, *Ghadah al-Samman,* 33.

29. Ghadah al-Samman, *al-a'mal ghayr al-kamila: saffarat indhar dakhil ra'si* (Beirut: Manshurat Ghadah al-Samman, 1980), 83.

30. Ibid., 81.

31. Ghadah al-Samman, "al-thawra al-jinsiyya wa'l-thawra al-shamila," *al-Mawaqif,* vol. 2, no. 12 (1970), 69.

32. Ibid., 71.

33. al-Samman, *al-a'mal ghayr al-kamila,* 226–28.

34. Ibid., 225.

35. Rossana Rossanda, "A Feminine Culture," in Monique Gadant, ed. (translated from the French by A. M. Berrett), *Women of the Mediterranean* (London: Zed Books, 1986), 187

36. Ibid., 183.

37. Shaaban, *Both Right and Left Handed*.

38. Ibid., 5. — Shaaban's graphic description of this incident underlines the inhuman dimension of the honor code as applied to women who commit, or are suspected of committing, premarital sex. As a literary theme in modern Arabic literature, the honor code has generally been presented in negative terms by male writers. But an increasing number of women writers have recently addressed themselves to this highly sensitive issue by voicing their opposition to the code as enforced violently against women. See, e.g., "Washing off Disgrace," a poem by Nazik al-Mala'ika, a leading poetess from Iraq (*Women of the Fertile Crescent*, edited with translation by Kamal Boullata [Washington, D.C.: Three Continent Press, 1978], 20 – 21). Ghadah al-Samman's short essay, "Women or 'Murderers,'" attacks the crime of honor as committed not by men, but by a young woman who seeks to murder her sister to protect her family's honor. The episode, rarely encountered in the literature, is depicted by al-Samman as "masculinized behavior," which certain liberated women display in pursuit of their emancipation. See al-Samman, *al-a'mal ghayr al-kamila*, 80–82.

39. Shaaban, *Both Right and Left Handed*, 5.

40. Ibid., 10–11.

41. Ibid., 236–37.

42. Ibid., 25.

43. Ibid., 15.

44. Ibid., 26–27.

45. See, for example Francine du Plessex Gray, *Soviet Women Walking the Tightrope* (Garden City, N.Y.: Doubleday, 1989), esp. 28–39, 114–31. Examples cited as negative in their orientation include the following passage by Tawfiq al-Hakim: "Women by their very nature master the pursuit of minute details in the affairs of daily life. . . . They have an inborn disposition for prolixity in narration . . . and a skill in holding a pen, weaving with it a tale about an individual, just as they are skillful in holding a needle to knit a dress. . . . But rarely can a woman become a writer of a profound culture and a sharp mind capable of dealing with mankind in discerning fashion or grasping fully the problems of her age or influencing the thinking of her time" (ibid., 45). Other passages that emphasize women's absolute obedience to their husbands or their domestic role include: "Be in agreement with him as much as possible and you will ensure his lasting companionship" (p. 88), and "The kitchen is the place where the housewife spends many hours" (p. 114). According to the author, these and similar passages, presented without any comment or discussion, serve to perpetuate women's subservient position and the responsibilities traditionally assigned to them.

Chapter 7. The Nature of the Soviet-Syrian Link

1. For Rubinstein's definition of influence, see his *Red Star on the Nile* (Princeton: Princeton University Press, 1977), xiv.

2. A copy of the full public text of the treaty was published in *Current Digest of the Soviet Press* (Columbus, Ohio), vol. 32, no. 41, 6.

3. See Ze'ev Schiff, "Green Light, Lebanon," in *Foreign Policy*, no. 50, Spring 1983: 75.

4. Author's interviews with former officials who asked not to be named, March 1987 and March 1988.

5. For details of the events leading up to this outcome, see Helena Cobban, *The Making of Modern Lebanon* (London: Hutchinson, and Boulder, Colo.: Westview, 1985), 196–206.

6. See, e.g., the references to Syria in Karen Brutents, *National Liberation Revolutions Today* (Moscow: Progress Publishers, 1977), vol. 2, p. 108; and idem, *The Newly-Free Countries in the Seventies* (Moscow: Progress Publishers, 1983), 147.

7. *Foreign Broadcasts Information Service—Soviet Union* (hereafter *FBIS-SU*), April 28, 1987: H7.

8. Interview with Igor Belyayev, Moscow, July 1988.

9. Author's interviews with officials and analysts in Moscow, July 1988.

10. Author's interview with a Western military source, summer 1987.

11. Quoted in Caryle Murphy, "Syria urged to stress defense," *The Washington Post*, November 20, 1989, A1, A28. "Reasonable defense sufficiency" was the principle according to which the Soviets had been trying to downsize their own military force structure since 1987.

12. "Official views Arab-USSR, Arab-U.S. relations," *Al-Watan* (Kuwait), Jan. 7, 1990: 18; as translated in *FBIS-SU90-006*, January 9, 1990: 33.

13. Damascus radio in Arabic, March 8, 1988; as translated in *FBIS-NES*, March 10, 1988: 55.

14. "President Hafiz al-Asad gives interview to U.S. newspapers," on Damascus television, August 14, 1983; as translated in *Joint Publications Research Service* (hereafter *JPRS*), 84191: 63.

15. "Al-Asad interviewed by U.S. columnist Evans," on Damascus television, Nov. 15, 1983; as translated in *FBIS-ME*, Nov. 16, 1983: H1.

16. Author's interview with Farouq al-Sharaa, July 1987.

17. Ibid.

18. For details and discussion of Israel's nuclear program, see "How Israel got the bomb," in *Time,* April 12, 1976: 39–40; Louis Rene Beres, *Security or Armageddon; Israel's Nuclear Strategy* (Lexington, Mass.: Lexington Books, 1986); and "Revealed: the secrets of Israel's nuclear arsenal," in *The Sunday Times* (London), Oct. 5, 1986: 1–3 passim.

19. Author's interview with Mustafa Tlas, July 1987.

20. "Al-Asad stresses need for self-reliance, strategic balance with Israel," in *Al Mustaqbal* (Paris), no. 298, Nov. 2, 1982: 19; as translated in *JPRS,* 82403: 148.

21. As quoted in Elisabeth Picard, "L'USSR vue par les Ba'thistes d'Iraq et de Syrie," in *L'USSR vue du tiers-monde* (Paris: Karthala, 1984), 84n.

22. Interview with Mustafa Tlas, in *Der Spiegel* (Hamburg), Sept. 22, 1986, 156–73; as translated in *FBIS-ME,* Sept. 23, 1986, H2.

23. Author's interview with Mustafa Tlas, July 1987.

24. Eric Rouleau, "Bluff or preparations for war?," in *Le Monde* (Paris), May 26, 1983, 1, 3; as translated in *FBIS-ME,* June 1, 1983, H1.

25. See Kassem M. Ja'far, "The Soviet Union in the Middle East: a Case Study of Syria," in Robert Cassen, ed., *Soviet Interests in the Third World* (London: Royal Institute of International Affairs, and Beverly Hills: Sage, 1985), 255–83; and Saadet Deger, "Soviet arms sales to developing countries: the economic forces," in ibid., 159–76.

26. *Middle East Economic Digest* (London), March 12, 1988, 29.

27. See Youssef M. Ibrahim, "Syria, for the first time, plans to export oil," in *The New York Times,* March 16, 1988, A9.

28. Another interesting question to ponder in this context is the potential strategic value of Israel, with its highly trained armed forces and developed military-industrial manufacturing infrastructure; but for the time being, the only realistic goal for the Soviets with respect to Israel must be to maximize their ability to curtail its benefit to the United States, rather than to seek to profit from it themselves.

29. For details, see "How Israel got the bomb," *New York Times,* March 16, 1988; and Henry Kissinger, *Years of Upheaval* (Boston: Little, Brown, 1982), 491–591 passim.

30. References to texts of relevant party congress reports.

31. Primakov's talk at Brookings, December 1987.

32. Karen Brutents, *National Liberation Revolutions Today* (Moscow: Progress Publishers, 1977), vol. 2, 108.

33. Karen Brutents, *The Newly-Free Countries in the Seventies* (Moscow: Progress Publishers, 1983), 90.

34. Ibid., 147.

35. Ibid., 100.

36. See Brutents' articles in *Pravda*, February 2, 1982, 4–5 (translated in *FBIS-SU*, Feb. 10, 1982, CC5–10); and *Pravda*, January 10, 1986, 3, 4 (translated in *FBIS-SU*, Jan. 14, 1986, CC2–7).

37. For details of some of these lessons, see Helena Cobban, "The lessons the Soviets learned from Israel's June 1982 strikes against Syrian ground-based air defenses in Lebanon," in David R. Jones, ed., *Soviet Armed Forces Review Annual*, no. 10 (forthcoming).

38. See report on the new Soviet FST-1 tank in *Newsweek*, April 1988.

39. For one clear exposition of such a warning, see V. A. Kremenyuk, "The United States in regional conflicts," in *SShA: Ekonomika, Politika, Ideologiya* (Moscow), no. 6, June 1986, 23–33; as translated in *JPRS*, USA 86-009, 25–37.

40. Syrian officials' concerns about the credibility of former Soviet commitments must have been further heightened when they saw the Soviets stand aside as popular movements in Eastern Europe toppled all the pro-Soviet governments there in the last months of 1989.

41. Ephraim Karsh, in the conclusion to his forthcoming book on Soviet-Syrian relations, MS 180.

BIBLIOGRAPHY

Abu Jaber, Kemal S. *The Arab Ba'th Socialist Party*. Syracuse: Syracuse University Press, 1966.

Abyad, Malikah. "Values of Syrian Youth: A Study Based on Syrian Students in Damascus University." M. A. thesis, American University of Beirut, 1968.

Accad, Evelyne. *Veil of Shame: The Role of Women in the Contemporary Fiction of North Africa and Arab World*. Sherbrook, Quebec: Naaman, 1978.

al-Akhras, Muhammad S. *Revolutionary Change and Modernization in the Arab World*. Damascus: 1972

———. *tarkib al-a'ila al-arabiyya wa waza'ifuha*. Damascus: 1976.

al-Alawi, Ali Aziz Ibrahim. *Alawis: the Unknown Shi'a Martyrs* (in Arabic). Damascus: no date.

Allan, J. A. "Syria's Agricultural Options." In J. A. Allan, ed., *Politics and the Economy in Syria*. London: School of Oriental and African Studies, University of London, 1987.

Allush, Naji. *al-thawra wa al-jamahir*. Beirut: Dar al-Talia, 1962.

Altoma, Salih J. "Westernization and Islam in Modern Arabic Fiction." *Yearbook of Comparative and General Literature* 20 (1970):81–88.

———. "Sociopolitical Themes in the Contemporary Arabic Novel: 1950 – 1970." In H. E. Lewald, ed., *The Cry of Home: Cultural Nationalism and the Modern Writer*. Knoxville: University of Tennessee Press, 1972, 351–73.

Amin, Samir. *Unequal Development—An Essay on the Social Formations of Peripheral Capitalism*. Translated by Brian Pearce. New York: Monthly Review Press, 1976.

Apter, D., ed. "Political Religion in the New Nations." In Clifford Geertz, ed., *Old Societies and New States*.

al-Asad, R. *The Economic, Social and Political Development in the Syrian Arab Region Between the National Revolution and the Class Revolution 1946 – 1963* (in Arabic). Damascus: Ad-Dar Al-Wataniyyah Distributions, 1973.

149

Awwad, Hanan Ahmad. *Arab Causes in the Fiction of Ghadah al-Samman (1961 –1975)*. Sherbrook, Quebec: Naaman, 1983.

Ayyash, Sami. *The Isma'ilis in the Qaramita Period* (in Arabic). Beirut: Dar Ibn Khaldun, no date.

Balandier, G. *Political Anthropology*. Middlesex: Penguin Books, 1970.

Barakat, Halim. *Visions of Social Reality in the Contemporary Arab Novel*. Washington, D.C.: 1977.

———. "The Arab Family and the Challenge of Social Transformation." In Elizabeth W. Fernea, ed., *Women and the Family in the Middle East: New Voices of Change*, 27–48.

Batatu, Hanna. *The Old Social Classes and the Revolutionary Movement of Iraq*. Princeton: Princeton University Press, 1978.

———. "Class Analysis and Iraqi Society." *Arab Studies Quarterly* 1 (Summer 1979): 229–40.

———. "Some Observations on the Social Roots of Syria's Ruling Military Group and the Causes for its Dominance." *The Middle East Journal*, vol. 35, no. 3 (Summer 1981): 331–44.

———. "Syria's Muslim Brethren." *MERIP Reports*, no. 110, 12 (November-December 1982).

Ben-Tzur, Avarham. "What Is Arab Socialism." *New Outlook*, vol. 8, no. 5 (1965): 37–45.

———. "The Neo-Ba'th Party of Syria." *Journal of Contemporary History* 18 (1968): 165–72.

Beres, Louis Rene. *Security or Armageddon: Israel's Nuclear Strategy*. Lexington, Mass.: Lexington Books, 1986.

Bourdieu, P. *Outline of a Theory of Practice*. Translated from the French by Richard Nice. Cambridge: Cambridge University Press, 1977.

Brutents, Karen. *National Liberation Revolutions Today*. Moscow: Progress Publishers, 1977, vol. 2.

———. *Pravda* (February 2, 1982): 4, 5.

———. *The Newly Free Countries in the Seventies*. Moscow: Progress Publishers, 1983.

———. *Pravda* (January 10, 1986): 3, 4.

Burke III, Edmund. "A Comparative View of French Native Policy in Morocco and Syria, 1912–1925." *Middle Eastern Studies* 9 (May 1973): 175–86.

Chevalier, Louis. *Classes Laborieuses et Classes Dangereuses à Paris pendant la Première Moitié du XIX Siècle*. Paris: Plon, 1958.

Cobban, Helena. "The Lessons the Soviets Learned from Israel's June 1982 Strikes against Syrian Ground-based Air Defenses in Lebanon." In David R. Jones, ed., *Soviet Armed Forces Review Annual* 10 (forthcoming).

Commins, David. "Religious Reformers and Arabists in Damascus, 1885–1914." *International Journal of Middle East Studies* 18 (November 1986): 405–25.

Cooke, Miriam. "Beirut — Theatre of the Absurd — Theatre of Dreams: The Lebanese Civil War in the Writings of Contemporary Arab Women." *Journal of Arabic Literature* 13 (1982): 124–41.

———. "Telling Their Lives: A Hundred Years of Arab Women's Writings." *World Literature Today* 60 (1986): 212–16.

Coon, Carleton. *Caravan: The Story of the Middle East*. New York: Holt, 1951.

Current Digest of the Soviet Press, vol. 32, no. 41:6.

Dawisha, Adeed. "Syria Under Asad, 1970–78: The Centres of Power." *Government and Opposition*, vol. 13, no. 3 (Summer 1978).

Dawn, C. Ernest. *From Ottomanism to Arabism: Essays on the Origins of Arab Nationalism*. Urbana: University of Illinois Press, 1973.

Deger, Saadet. "Soviet Arms Sales to Developing Countries: The Economic Force." In Robert Cassen, ed., *Soviet Interests in the Third World*. London: Royal Institute of International Affairs, and Beverly Hills: Sage, 1985, 159–76.

Der Spiegel. Hamburg (September 22, 1986): 156–73.

Devlin, John. *The Ba'th Party: A History from its Origins to 1966*. Stanford: Hoover Institution Press, 1976.

Drysdale, Alasdair. "Ethnicity in the Syrian Officer Corps." *Civilizations* 29 (1979): 359–74.

———. "The Syrian Political Elite, 1966–76: A Spatial and Social Analysis." *Middle Eastern Studies*, vol. 17, no. 1 (1981): 3–30.

———. "Regional Growth and Change in Syria since 1963." In J. A. Allan, ed., *Politics and the Economy in Syria*.

———. "The Regional Equalization of Health Care and Education in Syria Since the Ba'thi Revolution." *International Journal of Middle East Studies*, vol. 13 (1987): 93–111.

Dussaud, R. In E. Bouillon, ed., *Histoire et Religion des Nosairis*. Paris: 1900.

Farsoun, S., and Carroll, W. "State Capitalism and Counter-Revolution in the Middle East: A Thesis." In Barbara H. Kaplan, ed., *Social Change in the Capitalist World Economy.* Beverly Hills: Sage, 1978.

Fernea, Elizabeth W. *Women and the Family in the Middle East: New Voices of Change.* Austin: University of Texas Press, 1984.

Fernea, Elizabeth W., and Bezirgan, Basima Q. *Middle East Muslim Women Speak.* Austin: University of Texas Press, 1977.

Foreign Broadcasts Information Service — Soviet Union (February 10, 1982): CC5–10.

——— —*ME* (June 1, 1983): H1.

——— —*ME* (November 16, 1983): H1.

——— —*Soviet Union* (January 14, 1986): CC2–7.

——— —*ME* (September 23, 1986): H2.

——— —*Soviet Union* (April 28, 1987): H7.

——— —*NES* (March 10, 1988): 55.

Gadant, Monique, ed. *Women of the Mediterranean.* London: Zed Books, 1986.

Geertz, Clifford, "The New Integrative Revolution: Primordial Sentiments and Civil Politics in the New States." In Clifford Geertz, ed., *Old Societies and New States.* New York: Free Press of Glencoe, 1963.

Ghorayeb, Rose. "May Ziadeh (1886–1941)." *Signs* 5 (1979): 375–82.

———. "Arab Feminine Literature Between 1850 and 1950." *Al Raida* 7 (May 1988): 4–5.

Haddad, Yvonne Y. "Traditional Affirmations Concerning the Role of Women as Found in Contemporary Arab Islamic Literature." In Jane I. Smith, ed., *Women in Contemporary Muslim Societies.* London: Associated Press, and Lewisburg: Bucknell University Press, 1980, 61–88.

Haim, Sylvia G. "Love in an Arab Climate." *Encounter,* vol. 50, no. 2 (February 1978): 86–91.

———. "The Situation of the Arab Woman in the Mirror of Literature." *Middle Eastern Studies* 17 (1981): 510–30.

Hanna, Abdulla. *al-haraka al-'ummaliyya fi suriyya wa lubnan 1900–1945.* Damascus: 1973.

Hijab, Nadia. *Womenpower: The Arab Debate on Women at Work.* Cambridge and New York: Cambridge University Press, 1988.

Hindness, B., and Hirst, P. *Pre-capitalist Modes of Production.* London: Routledge & Keegan Paul, 1975.

Hinnebusch, Raymond A. "Local Politics in Syria: Organization and Mobilization in Four Village Cases." *Middle East Journal,* vol. 30, no. 1 (Winter 1976): 1–24.

————. "Rural Politics in Ba'thist Syria: A Case Study of the Role of the Countryside in the Society in the Political Development of Arab Socialism." In Saad Eddin Ibrahim and Nicholas S. Hopkins, eds., *Arab Society in Transition.* Cairo: American University in Cairo Press, 1977.

————. "Party and Peasant in Syria." *Cairo Papers in Social Science,* vol. 3, no. 1 (November 1979).

————. "Rural Politics in Ba'thist Syria." *Review of Politics,* vol. 44, no. 1 (January 1982): 110–30.

————. "Syria under the Ba'th: State Formation in a Fragmented Society." *Arab Studies Quarterly,* vol. 4, no. 3 (Summer 1982): 177–99.

————. "Syria under the Ba'th: Social Ideology, Policy and Practice." In Laurence Michalak and Jeswald Salacuse, eds., *Social Legislation in the Contemporary Middle East.* Berkeley: University of California Press, 1986, 61–109.

————. "Syria." In Shireen Hunter, ed., *The Politics of Islamic Revivalism.* Bloomington: Indiana University Press, 1988, 39–55.

Hourani, Albert. *Syria and Lebanon: A Political Essay.* London: Oxford University Press, 1946.

————. "Ottoman Reform and the Politics of Notables." In William R. Polk and Richard L. Chambers, eds., *Beginnings of Modernization in the East: The Nineteenth Century.* Chicago: University of Chicago Press, 1968.

————. "Revolution in the Arab Middle East." In P. J. Vatikiotis, ed., *Revolution in the Middle East and Other Case Studies.* London: Allen & Unwin, 1972.

Hrieb, Aleddin Saleh. "The Influence of Sub-Regionalism (Rural Areas) on the Structure of Syrian Politics, 1920–73." Ph.D. dissertation, Georgetown University.

Hudson, Michael. *Arab Politics: The Search for Legitimacy.* New Haven: Yale University Press, 1977.

Ibrahim, Youssef M. "Syria, for the first time, plans to export oil." *New York Times* (March 16, 1988): A9.

Ja'far, Kassem M. "The Soviet Union in the Middle East, a Case Study of Syria." In Robert Cassen, ed., *Soviet Interests in the Third World.* London: Royal Institute of International Affairs, and Beverly Hills: Sage, 1985, 255–83.

Joint Publications Research Service 82403:148, "Al-Asad stresses need for self-reliance, strategic balance with Israel."

—— 84191:63, "President Hafiz al-Asad gives interview to U.S. newspapers."

—— USA 86-009:25–37.

al-Jundi, Sami. *al-Ba'th*. Beirut: Dar al Nahar, 1969.

Kaylani, S. M. "The Role of Agriculture in the Development of Syria, 1945–1960." M. A. thesis, American University in Beirut, 1964.

Khalidi, Rashid. "Social Factors in the Rise of the Arab Movement in Syria." In Said Amir Arjomand, ed., *From Nationalism to Revolutionary Islam*. Albany: SUNY Press, 1984.

Khalidi, Tarif. "Toccata and Fugue." *Middle East Forum* 37 (October 8, 1961): 21–24.

al-Khatib, Husam. "Prose Fiction in Syria 1937–1965 with Special Reference to Foreign Influences." Dissertation, University of Cambridge, 1969.

——. "hawl al-riwaya al-nisa'iyya fi suriyya." *al-Marifa*, nos. 166, 168, and 169 (December 1975, February 1976, and March 1976).

Khoury, Philip S. *Urban Notables and Arab Nationalism: The Politics of Damascus, 1860–1920*. Cambridge: Cambridge University Press, 1983.

——. "Syrian Urban Politics in Transition: The Quarters of Damascus During the French Mandate." *International Journal of Middle East Studies* 16 (November 1984): 507–40.

——. *Syria and the French Mandate: The Politics of Arab Nationalism, 1920–1945*. Princeton: Princeton University Press, 1987.

——. "A Reinterpretation of the Origins and Aims of the Great Syrian Revolt, 1925–1927." In George N. Atiyeh and Ibrahim M. Oweiss, eds., *Arab Civilization: Challenges and Responses*. Albany: SUNY Press, 1988.

Khuri, Fuad I. *The Leadership of the Martyr and the Leadership of the Hero: The Religious Organization of Sects and Minorities in the Arab World (imamat al-shahid wa imamat al-batal: tanthim al-dini lada al-tawa'if wa al-aqiliyat fi al-'alim al-arabi)*. Juni, Lebanon: University Publishing House, 1988.

——. *Imams and Emirs: State, Religion and Sect in Islam*. London: SaQi Books, 1990.

al-Khuri, Kulit. *ayyam ma'ah*. Beirut: 1959.

——. *layla wahida*. Beirut: 1961.

——. *wa marra sayf*. Damascus: 1975.

Kremenyok, V. A. "The United States in regional conflicts." In *SShA Ekono-mika, Politika, Ideliqiva,* Moscow, no. 6 (June 1986): 23–33.

Lammens, H. *Les Nosairis, Notes sur leur Histoire et leur Religion.* Etude, no. 16: 1899.

Lapidus, Ira M. *Muslim Cities in the Later Middle Ages.* Cambridge: Harvard University Press, 1967.

Leca, Jean. "Social Structure and Political Stability: Comparative Evidence from the Algerian, Syrian and Iraqi Cases." In Adeed Dawisha and I. William Zartman, ed., *Beyond Coercion: The Durability of the Arab State.* London: Croom Helm, 1988, 164–202.

Lemel, Harold. "Rural Social Services." In USAID, *Syria: Agricultural Sector Assessment,* vol. 5. Washington, D.C.: 1980.

Lewis, Norman N. "Syria: Land and People." In J. A. Allan, ed., *Politics and the Economy of Syria.*

———. *Nomads and Settlers in Syria and Jordan, 1800–1980.* Cambridge: Cambridge University Press, 1987.

Longrigg, S. H. *Syria and Lebanon Under French Mandate.* London: Oxford University Press, 1988.

Longuenesse, Elisabeth. "La Classe Ouvrière au Proche Orient: La Syrie." *Pensée,* no. 197 (February 1978): 120–32.

———. "The Class Nature of the State in Syria." *MERIP Reports,* vol. 9, no. 4 (1979): 3–11.

———. "The Syrian Working Class Today." *MERIP Reports,* vol. 15, no. 6 (July-August 1985): 17–24.

Maoz, Mohse. "Syria under Hafiz al-Asad: New Domestic and Foreign Policies." In *Jerusalem Papers on Peace Problems,* 1975.

———. "Hafiz al-Asad: A Political Profile." *Jerusalem Quarterly* 8 (1978).

al-mar'a al-arabiyya al-suriyya fi aqd al-mar'a al-dawli: 1975–1985. Union of the Syrian Women. Damascus: 1987.

Metral, Françoise. "Le Monde Rural Syrien à l'Ere des Réformes (1958–1978)." In André Raymond et al., *La Syrie d'Aujourd'hui.* Paris: CNRS, 1980, 69–89.

———. "State and Peasants in Syria: A Local View of a Government Irrigation Project." In Nicholas S. Hopkins and Saad Eddin Ibrahim, eds., *Arab Society: Social Science Perspectives.* Cairo: University of Cairo Press, 1987.

Middle East Economic Digest. London (March 12, 1988): 29.

Moore, Clement Henry. "On Theory and Practice Among the Arabs." *World Politics* 24 (October 1974): 106–26.

Mortimer, Mildred. "A Feminist Critique of the Algerian Novel of French Expression." In David F. Dorsey et al., eds., *Design and Intent in African Literature*. Washington, D.C.: 1979, 31–38.

Moussa-Mahmoud, Fatima. *Women in the Arabic Novel in Egypt*. Cairo: Quaderni dell'istituto italiano, 1976.

Muslih, Muhammad Y. *The Origins of Palestinian Nationalism*. New York: Columbia University Press, 1988.

al-Mustaqbal. Paris, no. 298 (November 2, 1982). "Al-Asad stresses need for self-reliance, strategic balance with Israel."

Nieger, C. "Choix de Documents sur le Territoire des Alaouites." In *Revue du Monde Musulman* 44 (March 1922): 57–68.

O'Laughlin, B. "Marxist Approaches in Anthropology." In J. Siegel, ed., *Annual Review of Anthropology*, vol. 4 (1975): 341–70.

Petran, Tabitha. *Syria*. London: Ernest Benn, 1972.

Picard, Elizabeth. "Clans Militaires et Pouvoir Ba'thiste en Syrie." *Orient,* Hamburg (1979): 49–62.

———. "Ouverture Économique et Renforcement Militaire en Syrie." *Oriente Moderne*, vol. 59, nos. 7–12 (1979): 663–76.

———. "L'Urss vue par les Ba'thistes d'Iraq et de Syrie." In *L'URSS vue du tiers-monde,* Paris: Karthala, 1984.

Qarqut, Dhuqan. *tatawwur al-haraka al-wataniyya fi suriyya, 1920–1939*. Beirut: 1975.

al-Qazzaz, Ayad. "Political Order, Stability and Officers: A Comparative Study of Iraq, Syria and Egypt from Independence to June, 1967." *Middle East Forum* (November 1963).

el-Rabie, Mahmoud B. "Women Writers and Critics in Modern Egypt (1888–1963)." Dissertation, University of London, 1965.

Rabinovich, Itamar. *Syria under the Ba'th 1963–66*. New York: Halstead Press, 1972.

Rabo, A. *Change on the Euphrates*. Stockholm: Studies in Social Anthropology, 1986.

Rafeq, Abdul-Karim. "The Social and Economic Structure of Bab-al-Musalla (al-Midan), Damascus, 1825–1875." In George N. Atiyeh and Ibrahim M.

Oweiss, eds., *Arab Civilization: Challenges and Responses*. Albany: SUNY Press, 1988.

Raymond, André. "La Syrie, du Royaume Arabe à l'Indépendance (1914 – 1946)." In André Raymond, ed., *La Syrie d'Aujourd'hui*. Paris: 1980.

Razzaz, Munif. *al-tajriba al-murra*. Beirut: Dar al-Ghandur, 1967.

Redfield, Robert. *Peasant Society and Culture*. Chicago: University of Chicago Press, 1956.

Roberts, David. "The Background and Role of the Baath Party." In J. A. Allan, ed., *Politics and the Economy in Syria*.

Rondot, Pierre. "Les Mouvements Nationalistes au Levant durant la Deuxième Guerre Mondiale (1939 – 1945)." In *La Guerre Méditerranée (1939 – 1945)*. Paris: 1971.

———. "L'expérience du Mandat Français en Syrie et au Liban (1918–45)." *Revue de Droit International Publique* 3–4 (1948): 387–409.

Rossanda, Rossana. "A Feminine Culture." In Monique Gadant, ed., *Women of the Mediterranean*. Translated from the French by A. M. Berrett, 182–96.

Rouleau, Eric. "Bluff or preparations for War?" *Le Monde,* Paris (May 26, 1983).

Rubinstein, Alvin. *Red Star on the Nile*. Princeton: Princeton University Press, 1977.

Sadowski, Yahya M. "The Knife's Edge: A Study of the Failure of Liberalization in Syria." Unpublished seminar paper. Los Angeles: University of California at Los Angeles, 1978.

———. "Cadres, Guns and Money: The Eighth Regional Congress of the Syrian Ba'th Party." *MERIP Reports,* vol. 15, no. 6 (July-August 1985): 3–8.

———. "Graft and the Ba'ath: Corruption and Control in Contemporary Syria." *Arab Studies Quarterly,* vol. 9 (Fall 1987): 422–61.

Safadi, Muta. *hizb al-ba'th*. Beirut: Dar al-Adab, 1964.

———. "A Feminine Culture." In Monique Gadant, ed., *Women of the Mediterranean*, 182–96.

Salamah, Ibrahim. *al-ba'th min al-mudaris ila al-thakanat*. Beirut: 1969.

Salame, G. *State and Society in the Arab East* (in Arabic). Beirut: Center of Arab Unity Studies, 1987.

al-Samman, Ghadah. *layla al-ghuraba.'* Beirut: 1966.

———. "al-thawra al-jinsiyya wa'l-thawra al-shamila." *al-Mawaqif,* vol. 2, no. 12 (1970): 68–73.

————. "The sexual revolution and the total Revolution." In Elizabeth W. Fernea and Basima Bezirgan, eds., *Middle Eastern Muslim Women Speak,* 391–99.

————. *al-a'mal ghayr al-kamila: saffarat indhar dakhil ra'si.* Beirut: 1980.

Sayyid, Jallal. *hizb al-ba'th al-arabi.* Beirut: Dar al-Nahar, 1973.

Schiff, Ze'ev. "Green Light, Lebanon." *Foreign Policy,* no. 50 (Spring 1983): 75.

Schilcher, Linda Schatkowski. *Families in Politics: Damascene Factions and Estates of the Eighteenth and Nineteenth Centuries.* Stuttgart: 1985.

Schipper, Mineke, ed. *Unheard Words: Women and Literature in Africa, the Arab World, Asia, the Caribbean and Latin America.* London and New York: 1984, 72–120.

Seale, Patrick. *The Struggle for Syria: A Study of Post-War Arab Politics.* London: Oxford University Press, 1965.

Seymour, Martin. "The Dynamics of Power in Syria since the Break with Egypt." *Middle Eastern Studies* 6, 1970.

Shaaban, Bouthaina. *Both Right and Left Handed: Arab Women Talk About Their Lives.* London: Women's Press, 1988.

al-Sharif, Munir. *The Alawi Muslims.* Damascus: Dar al-Umumiya, 1961.

Shukri, Ghali. *ghadah al-samman bila ajniha.* Beirut: 1977.

al-Siba'i, Badr al-Din. *adwa' 'ala al-rasmal al-ajnabi fi suriyya 1850–1958.* Damascus: 1958.

Sluglett, Peter, and Farouq-Sluglett, Marion. "The Application of the 1858 Land Code in Greater Syria: Some Preliminary Observations." In Tarif Khalidi, ed., *Land Tenure and Social Transformation in the Middle East.* Beirut: American University of Beirut, 1984.

Sulayman, Nabil. *al-niswiyya fi al-kitab al-suri al-madrasi 1967–1976.* Damascus: 1978.

Suleiman, Michael W. "Changing Attitudes Toward Women in Egypt: The Role of Fiction in Women's Magazines." *Middle Eastern Studies* 14 (1978): 352–71.

The Sunday Times, London. "Revealed: the secrets of Israel's nuclear arsenal." (October 5, 1986): 1–3.

Syrian Arab Republic (SAR). *1970–71 Agricultural Census Data: First Stage, Basic Data in Syrian Arab Republic.* Damascus: Central Bureau of Statistics, 1970–71.

————. *Agricultural Census Data, Second Stage, Detailed Data.* Damascus: Central Bureau of Statistics, 1971.

———. *Annual Statistical Bulletin of the Co-operative Sector [neshrat al-ihsa'lya sanawi lil-qita al-ta'awuni].* Damascus: Ministry of Agriculture, 1972.

———. *Statistical Abstract, 1984.* Damascus: Central Bureau of Statistics, 1984, 88, 94.

Tabari, Azar. "The Women's Movement in Iran: A Hopeful Progress." *Feminist Studies* 12 (1986): 343–60.

Tamer, Zakaria. *Tigers on the Tenth Day and Other Stories.* London: 1985.

al-Tawil, Mohammad Amin Ghaleb. *The History of the Alawis.* Beirut: Dar al-Andalus, 1966.

Teske, Raymond H. C., and Barden, H. Nelson. "Acculturation and Assimilation: A Clarification." *American Ethnologist,* vol. 1, no. 2 (May 1974): 351–67.

Time. "How Israel got the bomb." (April 12, 1976): 39–40.

Torrey, Gordon. "The Ba'th: Ideology and Practice." *Middle East Journal,* vol. 23, no. 4 (1969).

Uthman, Hashim. *The Alawis Between Myth and Reality* (in Arabic). Beirut: Mu'assassat al-A'lami, 1980.

Van Dam, Nikolas. *The Struggle for Power in Syria: Sectarianism, Regionalism, and Tribalism in Politics, 1961–1980.* London: Croom Helm, 1981.

Van Dusen, Michael H. "Intra- and Inter-Generational Conflict in the Syrian Army." Ph.D. dissertation, Johns Hopkins University, 1971.

———. "Downfall of a Traditional Elite." In Frank Tachau, ed., *Political Elites and Political Development in the Middle East.* Cambridge, Mass.: Schenkman/Wiley, 1975, 115–55.

Warriner, Doreen. *Land and Poverty in the Middle East.* London: 1948.

———. *Land Reform and Development in the Middle East.* London: 1962.

Weulersse, Jacques. *Paysan de Syrie et du Proche-Orient.* Paris: Gallimard, 1946.

World Bank. *Syrian Arab Republic: Development Prospects and Policies,* vol. 2, 90 (1980).

Youssef, Nadia. "The Status and Fertility Patterns of Muslim Women." In Lois Beck and Nikki Keddie, eds., *Women in the Muslim World.* Cambridge: Harvard University Press, 1978, 69–99.

Zaydan, Abdul-Karim. *The Individual and the State in Islamic Law* (in Arabic). Baghdad: Dar Salman al-A'zami, 1965.

CONTRIBUTORS

Salih Altoma is a poet and professor of Near Eastern languages and cultures at Indiana University. He received his B.A. from Baghdad University and his doctorate in language education from Harvard University. He has written *The Problem of Diglossia in Arabic* (Harvard University Press, 1969), *Palestinian Themes in Modern Arabic Literature: 1917–1970* (Cairo, 1972), collections of poetry, and numerous articles addressing sociopolitical themes in modern Arabic literature as well as the linguistic problems involved in teaching Arabic in secondary schools. He is currently writing a book tentatively entitled *The American Reception of Arabic Literature: 1900–1990*.

Richard T. Antoun is professor of anthropology at the State University of New York at Binghamton. He has conducted research among peasants and post-peasants in Jordan, Iran, and Lebanon, focusing on religion, kinship, law, and local politics. His books include *Arab Village* (Indiana University Press, 1972), *Low-Key Politics* (SUNY Press, 1979), and *Muslim Preacher in the Modern World* (Princeton University Press, 1989). His current research focuses on the impact of migration abroad for education and work from Jordan to Arabia, Europe, North America, and Asia.

Helena Cobban is the author of *The Palestinian Liberation Organization: People, Power and Politics* (Cambridge University Press, 1984), and *The Making of Modern Lebanon* (Westview Press, 1985). A member of the International Institute for Strategic Studies, she has also written extensively on the involvement of the United States and the Soviet Union in the Arab-Israeli military theater, including "The U.S.-Israeli relationship in the Reagan era," in *Conflict Quarterly,* Spring 1989; "A Blind Eye to Nuclear Proliferation" (co-authored with Gerard C. Smith), in *Foreign Affairs,* Summer 1989; and an examination of changes in Soviet policy under Gorbachev, "Ending Bloodshed in the Third World," in *World Monitor* (Boston), December 1988.

Raymond Hinnebusch is associate professor of political science at the College of St. Catherine, St. Paul, Minnesota. He is the author of numerous articles on Syria and a two-volume study of the Ba'th regime entitled *Peasant and Bureaucracy in Ba'thist Syria* (Westview Press, 1989) and *Authoritarian Power and State Formation in Ba'thist Syria: Army, Party, and Peasant* (Westview Press, 1990).

Sulayman Khalaf is assistant professor of anthropology in the Department of Sociology and Social Work, Kuwait University, Kuwait. He received his B.A. and M.A. from the American University of Beirut and his Ph.D. in anthropology in 1981 from the University of California, Los Angeles. He has done fieldwork research on beduins and peasants in the context of social change in Syria, and has written a number of articles on sociocultural change in Kuwait. He is currently involved in anthropological research on the dynamics of sociocultural change in Kuwait and the larger Arab Gulf societies.

Philip Khoury is professor of history and associate dean of the School of Humanities and Social Science at the Massachusetts Institute of Technology. He is the author of *Urban Notables and Arab Nationalism* (Cambridge University Press, 1983) and *Syria and the French Mandate* (Princeton University Press, 1987), which was awarded the George Louis Beer Prize of the American Historical Association. He is also co-editor of *Tribes and State Formation in the Middle East* (University of California Press, 1990). Professor Khoury's current research focuses on war and society in the twentieth-century Middle East. He is presently editing, with Albert Hourani and Mary C. Wilson, *A Modern Middle East History Reader.*

Fuad Khuri is a prominent Lebanese anthropologist currently living and working in Reading, England. He has conducted research in West Africa, Lebanon, Bahrain, Yemen, and Oman. His books include *An Eye on Lebanon* (in Arabic, 1964), *From Village to Suburb: Order and Change in Greater Beirut* (University of Chicago Press, 1975), *Tribe and State in Bahrain* (University of Chicago Press, 1980), *Imams and Emirs: State, Religion, and Sect in Islam* (Saqi Books, 1990), and *Tents and Pyramids: Games and Ideology in Arab Culture from Backgammon to Autocratic Rule* (Saqi Books, 1991).

Donald Quataert is associate professor of history and Director of the Southwest Asia and North Africa Program at the State University of New York at Binghamton. He is the author of *Social Disintegration and Popular Resistance in the Ottoman Empire 1881–1908* (New York University Press, 1983), *Technology Transfer and Manufacturing in the Middle East 1750–1914* (forthcoming), and *Home, Workshop, and Factory Manufacturing in the Ottoman Middle East 1800–1914* (forthcoming). His current research focuses on artisans and popular revolts in the Ottoman Empire from the seventeenth through the nineteenth centuries.

Patrick Seale is a British author and journalist specializing in Middle East affairs. His books include *The Struggle for Syria* (Oxford University Press, 1965; republished by Yale University Press, 1986) and *Asad: The Struggle for the Middle East* (University of California Press, 1988). He is now researching a project on the politics of the Palestinian resistance movement.

INDEX

Administration of Syria: map, xxi;
under Hafiz al-Asad, 101–102
Aflaq, Michel, 98–99
aghas (military chiefs), 15–16
Alawis, xv, 7–10, 26–27, 31, 31–35,
41–42, 97, 107, 109, 139n; elite, 43,
45; and military, 46; power of, 11;
and religious ideology and
organization, 49–61 passism; and
stratified view of religion, 53–57;
theological beliefs of, 9, 51–57; and
tribal structure, 60
Aleppo, viii, 15, 19, 36, 102, 108,
139n; population of, xix, 2
Arab nationalism, vii, 3, 18–19, 21,
134n; and pan-Arabism, 118
Army, 27; Ba'thization of, 35; officers,
31–32, 34; Syrian, 8–9, 26, 109
Asad, Hafiz al-, xiii, 6, 27, 35, 77, 97–
110 passim; and Gorbachev, 111–
129 passim; and intra-party coup,
36; and leadership style, 105–106;
and policy of strategic balance,
115–116; as religious leader, 61; and
state formation, 39–42, 47, 104
ashraf (descendants of the Prophet),
15

Ba'th Party, vii, xv, 3, 26, 35, 63, 71;
and agriculture, 37–38; and army,
33; and central committee, 100; and
corrective movement, 77–78; and
Hafiz al-Asad, 98; institutions of,
99–101; and Marxism-Leninism,
33, 46; and neo-Ba'thists, 64, 71–

72, 75, 77–78, 99; origins of, 30–33;
philosophy of, 80; radical, 29, 47,
74; and reforms, 36–39; and
regional command, 99; and
relations with the state, 101–105;
and revolution from above, 33–36;
and women, 81
Batatu, Hanna, viii, 7, 9, 25
Bitar, Salah al-Din, 98
Bourdieu, Pierre, 69
Britain and Syria, xiii

Capitalism, 68; and
entrepreneurialism, 69; and state
formation, 31
Carter, Jimmy: and Camp David
diplomacy, 113, 115
Christianity, 51; and Christian rituals,
50
Circassians, 1
Class/es in Syria, 1, 38–39, 141n; and
the bourgeoise, 35, 39–40, 44; and
Ba'th Party, 33; and conflict, 30–
33, 47; and land reform, 63–77
passim; lower middle, 26, 33; and
middle class radicalism, 33; models
of, 3; new middle, 31; and sects,
46–47; and the state, 29–47 passim;
Syrian upper, 18; urban middle, 34,
40
Cleveland, William, viii
Coon, Carleton, 2
Culture: and honor, 86, 145n; Syrian
political, 13–27 passim

163